D0513581

COOKING
JAPANESE-STYLE

MARK GREGORY & YUZABURO MOGI

 **MARTIN BOOKS**

 **KIKKOMAN**

Published by Martin Books
Simon & Schuster International Group
Fitzwilliam House, 32 Trumpington Street, Cambridge CB2 1QY

in association with
Kikkoman Corporation
1–25 Kanda Nishiki-cho
Chiyoda-ku
Tokyo 101
Japan

First published 1990
Text © Mark Gregory and Yuzaburo Mogi 1990
Photographs © Woodhead-Faulkner (Publishers) Ltd 1990

ISBN 0 85941 622 4

All rights reserved. No part of this publication may be reproduced, stored in
a retrieval system or transmitted, in any form or by any means, electronic,
mechanical, photocopying or otherwise, without the prior permission of the
copyright owners. CIP data available.

Design: Ken Vail Graphic Design, Cambridge
Photography: Laurie Evans
Styling: Lesley Richardson
Food preparation for photography: Mark Gregory with Sandra Baddeley
Calligraphy: Kaoru Miyake
Authentication: Tomi Shino

Printed and bound in Great Britain by Richard Clay Ltd, Bungay, Suffolk

NOTES ON RECIPES

Ingredients are given in both metric and imperial measures. Use either set of
quantities, but not a mixture of both in any one recipe.
All spoon measures are level:
1 tablespoon = one 15 ml spoon
1 teaspoon = one 5 ml spoon
Eggs are standard (size 3) unless otherwise stated.

CONTENTS

Foreword   4

Introduction   7

Japanese naturally-brewed soy sauce   8

Glossary   10

一 SOUPS AND SAUCES   12

二 COLD FIRST COURSES   23

三 HOT FIRST COURSES   37

四 FISH DISHES   50

五 MEAT DISHES   62

六 VEGETABLE, RICE AND TOFU DISHES   78

七 SALADS   92

八 SWEETS   99

Japanese ingredients suppliers   111

Index   112

FOREWORD

When I first saw the pictures of Mark's work for the British Chef of the Year Competition which he won in 1988, I knew that he would be the eventual successor to Britain's famous Anton Mosiman, and that he was walking in the footsteps of Japan's most revered owner-chef, Kihachi Kumagai of Kihachi Restaurant, Tokyo.

Mark had already come to my attention through his work in Australia and New Zealand, where he became Chef of the Year in 1987. This part of the world is a prime market for Kikkoman soy sauce, and when Mark came to Britain it coincided with the launch of our soy sauce on the UK market.

I have wanted to cooperate with this talented chef whose use of fresh vegetables, fruit and fish, and meticulous care with presentation, reflects the Japanese reverence for good food beautifully presented.

My own family has been involved in the production of the best accompaniment to good food – naturally fermented soy sauce – for $3^1/2$ centuries. Soy sauce was brought to Japan by the influence of Chinese Buddhism over fifteen hundred years ago. This new religion forbade the use of meat- and fish-based sauces which we had traditionally used to flavour our food. Thus soy sauce became a popular seasoning in Japan. The Chinese used only soybeans in producing their sauces. As the art of soy sauce-making gradually developed in Japan, we added wheat to the mixture to make the sauce more aromatic and flavoursome. Today Kikkoman soy sauce is made from these original ingredients: soybeans, wheat, salt and water.

When Dutch and Portuguese traders reached

The Kikkoman Imperial soy sauce plant

our shores in the seventeenth century, they prized soy sauce above any other condiment, and shipped it back to Europe in barrels and ceramic jars. Coloured blue and grey, these soy sauce jars are precious museum exhibits today. Eventually, as soy sauce was traded throughout Europe, it reached France, and was taken to the court of Louis XIV, who called it 'liquid spice' and that is how it has been known ever since.

The Mogi family came into sauce-making in 1630, near Noda City on the banks of the Edo River, where ample supplies of soybeans and wheat were available. In those days our sauce was shipped on river rafts to the great city of Edo, known today as Toyko. We adopted as our symbol the shell of the turtle, which is considered in Japan to be a creature of great good fortune and longevity. Thus the hexagon which appears on all our products implies good luck, and the calligraphy inside the hexagon reads 10,000 years, which can be interpreted as signifying good fortune and success in business.

This symbol is familiar to every household in Japan. Today we produce 340 million litres of soy sauce per year and still make soy sauce for the Imperial household of Japan in a special factory built to look like a traditional castle surrounded by a moat.

To make our sauce the soybeans and wheat are mixed together and a 'koji' starter is added. Literally translated, 'koji' means 'bloom of mould' – ours is named 'aspergillus sojae'. As the 'koji' mixture grows over a 45-hour period, special enzymes vital to the final flavour and colour of the sauce begin to form. Next we add a salt water solution to the 'koji' mixture, and allow it to ferment naturally for six months. The resultant brew is called a 'mature mash' and has a smooth, reddish-brown liquid appearance. For the Imperial table, we brew the mash in open, red wooden vats; for the consumer market we use modern stainless steel vessels, but the process is exactly the same. The mash is pressed between layers of cloth and clear soy sauce is extracted, which we pasteurise and bottle.

Our naturally fermented soy sauce has some 280 different flavour and aroma components,

Vats in the Kikkoman Imperial soy sauce plant

such as the essence of flowers, herbs, spices, meat and fish – all derived from this one simple, natural process. All these sensations delicately mix and harmonise so that one does not dominate the others. Our special Kikkoman flavour enhances the natural taste of good food, never overpowering or dominating, but complementing fresh ingredients.

It is sad to see so many soy sauces on the market made from hydrolysed vegetable protein. Such products can be made in a matter of days by adding corn syrup, caramel and other artificial substances to chemically decomposed vegetable protein in order to form amino acids. To the Japanese palate, the difference between our natural soy sauce and its imitators is the same as that between fine wine and an indifferent blend. Our soy sauce is naturally fermented using soybeans, wheat, salt and water, and our expertise has taken $3^{1}/_{2}$ centuries to perfect.

I hope you enjoy the equally natural genius of Mark Gregory, and that these recipes, adapted from the Japanese by one of the West's greatest chefs, will bring you and your family pleasure for many years to come.

Yuzaburo Mogi
Executive Managing Director
Kikkoman Corporation

Yuzaburo Mogi was educated at Keio University, receiving a B.A. in 1958, the year he joined the Kikkoman Corporation. In 1961, he received an M.B.A. from Columbia Business School, and in 1977 joined the Board of Directors of Kikkoman Foods Inc., Wisconsin, U.S.A. He became Executive Managing Director of Kikkoman Corporation in 1989. He holds several trusteeships and directorships of organisations dedicated to the food industry and Japanese business relationships with foreign countries. He is also Honorary Ambassador of the State of Wisconsin. Mr Mogi lives in Tokyo with his wife and three children. His favourite pastimes are golf, travel and watching sporting events.

INTRODUCTION

My love affair with Asian cookery dates back to 1979 when, as an apprentice chef working in New Zealand, I met and later married my first wife, Jacqueline. Jacqueline is Eurasian and her mother, Ina, was to my delight a wonderful cook.

I remember to this day a particular chicken dish of my mother-in-law's. it was pot-roasted and served with potatoes and hoisin sauce. The aromatic smell and taste of that wonderful meal will live with me all my life.

Much of what Ina had learnt from her own mother was carefully passed on to Jacqueline. At home we ate Asian-style foods more often than not as Jacqueline loved to cook, and had inherited much of her mother's feeling for food. 'The way to a man's heart is through his stomach' was certainly true in our case!

My personal interest led to a professional one, and I became particularly interested in Japanese cookery which I found to be distinctive and different from the cookery of other Asian countries.

The minimalism which usually characterises Japanese design also appears in Japanese cuisine. The influences and flavours tend to be clean and uncluttered, and on the whole Japanese taste sensation is pure and unadulterated. Japan's culinary traditions remain relatively unchanged even in today's busy world.

Our need for good health and a balanced diet has been emphasised in nearly every Japanese cookbook I have read. It is widely believed that Japanese food is good for slimming too. This belief is only partly true: whether one has a European or Asian diet, it's the balance of the foods that provide each individual with good health and correct weight control. Many recipes in this book are naturally healthy because of their ingredients and simple methods of preparation and cooking. Vegetarians will find much of interest in the book, and many dishes well suited to their requirements.

Whilst the traditional Japanese recipes I have chosen remain unchanged and are as authentic as possible, other more accessible recipes reflect the widespread influence that Japanese cuisine has had on Western food. Included also are some recipes influenced by other Asian countries such as China and India, these are added purely because they taste good and are fun to prepare.

A useful tip, when using this or any other cookbook, is to read carefully your chosen recipe at least twice before starting. This advice was given to me as an apprentice chef and it has saved my day many times.

Soy sauce was first used in the Orient about 2,500 years ago. The Japanese refined it by adding wheat to the soy, water and salt mash, and now it plays as important a role in Asian countries as different stocks do in French cuisine. As naturally fermented soy sauce enhances the flavour of good foods without overpowering their natural taste, it is a necessity to include it in many recipes.

This leads me to thank the book's sponsors. Kikkoman soy sauce is a good quality combination of natural ingredients, which, after six months' fermentation, yields numerous aromatic flavours. It does not contain monosodium glutamate, artificial additives, preservatives or colourings. I have used it for six years, and have found it well pleases both my customers, family and readers. Eat well and be healthy.

Mark Gregory

JAPANESE NATURALLY-BREWED SOY SAUCE

Every Japanese table bears a bottle or porcelain pot containing soy sauce. It is found in all types of restaurants – even top Chinese chefs turn to Japan when it comes to serving their customers with the best soy sauce. The famous Bullet Train speeding through the Japanese countryside carries Bento Boxes – a range of beautifully produced picnic meals, pre-packed with care, in colourful cardboard outers. Inside are portions of rice, fish or meat, pickles, wooden disposable chopsticks, and a miniature container of soy sauce. Soy sauce is as indispensable to the Japanese housewife as pepper, salt, mustard and vinegar are to the Western household.

To understand why the Japanese treasure their national sauce rather as the French revere their fine wines, one has to understand the soy sauce-making process, which is very similar to that of wine-making.

Nowhere is this better demonstrated than inside Goyogura, the Imperial soy sauce plant built on the banks of the Edo river. Kikkoman has long held the honour of being the official supplier of soy sauce to the Imperial household, and it is made in a building styled to look like an ancient castle. A group of white-walled buildings with steep-pitched tiled roofs cluster around a central cobbled courtyard. The plant is reached by a red painted bridge spanning a deep moat. Blossoming trees, lily pads, gold and silver carp, and a pair of stately swans – a gift from the Imperial Park – complete the typical Japanese scene.

The Goyogura brewers uphold traditional methods that have been handed down for three and a half centuries. This sketch illustrates the process. First, top quality soybeans are selected and steamed, then mixed with golden kernels of roasted, crushed wheat in roughly equal proportions. Yeast is added to start the natural fermentation process. Kikkoman use their own special starter called 'aspergillus sojae', which has formed the basis of their product's success for generations. After three days the soy and wheat mixture grows a mould or culture over the surface, at which stage it is referred to as 'koji'. The mixture is now ready for blending with salted water, and the resultant wet mash, called 'moromi', is put into fermentation tanks or vats.

Over a period of weeks the 'moromi' mixture bubbles gently as the soybean protein changes to amino acids, giving that special taste to the finished sauce. Wheat starch changes to sugar, and the mixture of amino acids and sugar form the natural colour of the sauce. The sugar content gradually changes to alcohol, yielding a distinctive aroma. Some of the alcohol and sugar transforms into various acids, giving tartness to the final flavour. The mixture matures after six months, then is drawn off into cloths to be pressed. A deep reddish-brown clear liquid is funnelled from the pressing machines to be pasteurised and bottled ready for shipping to over 80 countries around the world.

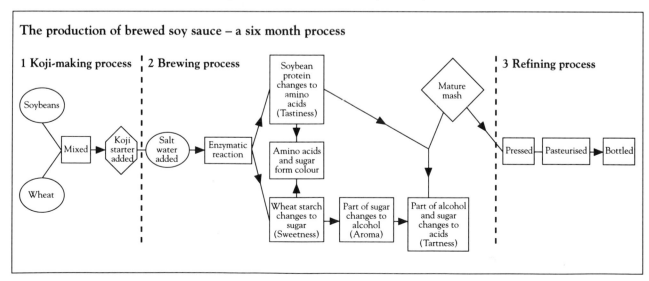

The production of brewed soy sauce – a six month process

1 Koji-making process | 2 Brewing process | 3 Refining process

Soybeans → Mixed ← Wheat → Koji starter added → Salt water added → Enzymatic reaction → Soybean protein changes to amino acids (Tastiness) / Amino acids and sugar form colour / Wheat starch changes to sugar (Sweetness) → Part of sugar changes to alcohol (Aroma) → Part of alcohol and sugar changes to acids (Tartness) → Mature mash → Pressed → Pasteurised → Bottled

Non-brewed soy sauce

The Japanese are rather scathing about the vast number of poor quality soy sauces currently on the market. Many of these are made in just three days. Plant proteins are mixed with hydrochloric acid, then boiled, cooled and neutralised with carbon soda. The resultant liquid is called hydrolised vegetable protein. Caramel, artificial flavourings, salt and water are added to make a non-brewed soy sauce.

The taste test

Like fine wine, naturally brewed soy sauce should be treated with the care its long preparation deserves. After opening, the cap should be tightly closed and the bottle kept in the refrigerator or a cool pantry. High temperature and direct exposure to air over a period of time causes oxidisation so that the sauce may lose flavour and aroma, and the colour can darken somewhat.

The Japanese have an infallible test for good soy sauce – they pour the sauce neat into a small porcelain bowl and taste it. Only naturally brewed soy sauce can be enjoyed in this manner. Artificially produced sauces will be too harsh on the tongue and palate to pass the taste test.

The heritage, history and skill that go into the product have made naturally brewed soy sauce the most popular seasoning throughout the world wherever fresh food and good cooking are appreciated.

Kikkoman naturally-brewed soy sauce, and Kikkoman Teriyaki sauce

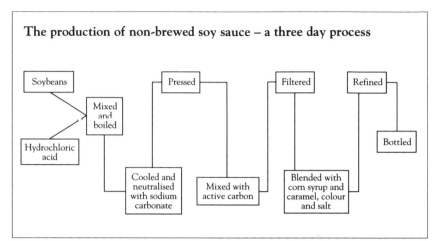

The production of non-brewed soy sauce – a three day process

Soybeans → Mixed and boiled ← Hydrochloric acid

Mixed and boiled → Pressed / Cooled and neutralised with sodium carbonate

Pressed / Cooled and neutralised with sodium carbonate → Mixed with active carbon

Filtered / Mixed with active carbon → Blended with corn syrup and caramel, colour and salt

Refined / Blended with corn syrup and caramel, colour and salt → Bottled

GLOSSARY

Asian lily flowers, dried
Used for chicken, pork and fish dishes.

Bean shoots
Often added to salads, stir-fries, one-pot dishes and soups.

Beanthread (harusame)
Most commonly made from mung beans, these fine, translucent filaments, which look like noodles, are softened in boiling water for 5–10 minutes before use. Often added to vinegared dishes, and one-pot dishes cooked at the table.

Birds' nest
This is the edible nesting material of a kind of swift. It is a solidified gelatinous mass of birds' saliva, from which all vegetation has been removed. It is available dried.

Bonito flakes
The bonito is a large game fish from which four main fillets are taken, and air-dried into blocks (katsuo-bushi). These are thinly shaved immediately before use, and are sometimes mixed with kelp to make basic soup stock (dashi, below). Packaged bonito flakes (hana-katsuo or kezuri-katsuo) are acceptable alternatives to make dashi, and can be sprinkled over soups, salads and cooked vegetables.

Chilli oil
This is a hot seasoning for noodles, dressings, meat and fish dishes.

Daikon
Known as mouli in the West, this is a giant white radish. Often used grated as a condiment, for Tempura dipping sauce, mixed with grated ginger, finely sliced to garnish Sashimi, or diced or sliced in boiled dishes.

Dashi
This is a basic stock (see page 20). Primary dashi (ichiban dashi), for clear soup, is made from bonito flakes and giant kelp (konbu); secondary dashi (niban dashi) is for thick soups, noodle broth, casseroles and one-pot dishes, and is re-used ichiban dashi, or commercially made dashi. In konbu-dashi, suitable for vegetarians, the bonito flakes are omitted.

Hijiki seaweed
This is a black seaweed, and is used in salads and fish dishes, or cooked with thin strips of deep-fried tofu (abura-age).

Hoisin sauce
Often called barbecue sauce, this is a spicy condiment used in a wide range of dishes.

Konbu seaweed
This is an edible kind of dried giant kelp, usually mixed with bonito flakes, as the base for soups and one-pot dishes. It can be simmered in soy sauce and seasonings and used as a spicy side dish.

Lemon grass
A verbena-flavoured ingredient used in soups, sauces, marinades, fish and meat dishes.

Lotus root (renkon)
This is the root of the aquatic lotus plant, and is best soaked in water with a little vinegar before use.

Mirin
This is a rice wine for cooking, not drinking. It adds sweetness and a subtle flavour to boiled and grilled dishes. Sometimes a dry white wine or dry sherry can be substituted, although nothing really replaces the unique flavour of mirin.

Miso
There are many varieties of miso, a popular seasoning in Japanese cookery, which is made by fermenting soybeans. A very commonly-used ingredient in Japanese cookery, its composition varies depending on the type of malt added to the soybean mash: there is rice miso (kome-miso), barley miso (mugi-miso) and straight soybean miso (mame-miso).
The salt and starch content of miso is also varied. It is a flavouring for soups, sauces, meat and fish dishes, and one-pot dishes.

Nori seaweed
The leaves of a soft seaweed which are dried by toasting to form a delicious condiment. It is an essential ingredient in Sushi, and adds flavour to deep-fried dishes, soups and fish dishes.

Oyster sauce
Made from oyster extract, this is a speciality sauce used in fish dishes, soups and sauces, for stir-fry, with green beans or with rice. It is suitable for paella- or risotto-type dishes.

Pickled ginger, sweet and savoury
Widely used as an accompaniment to Sushi; also used in salads, dressings, fish and meat dishes.

Rice paper
This is used for the presentation of deep-fried food, and also in making desserts.

Rice vinegar
Essential for Sushi, this is also commonly used in dressings and sauces.

Saké
This is rice wine, the traditional accompaniment to a Japanese meal. The best grades of saké are for drinking (at blood temperature) and the lower grades are used in sauces, marinades and dressings.

Sansho pepper
This spice is from the jacket of the prickly ash seed, and gives a unique flavour to soups, eel dishes and other fish dishes.

Sesame seed oil
This has a rich flavour, and is used in dressings, sauces and marinades. It burns at a comparatively low temperature, so only add it to dishes when cooking is finished. For tempura (page 78) it is mixed with salad oil before frying.

Sesame seeds, black and white
Black, white or brown, these are used whole, or toasted and ground as a coating for deep-fried fish, meat and vegetables, dressings, and dipping sauces, or sprinkled over salads. White goma complements fruit dishes.

Shiitake mushrooms
These are aromatic black mushrooms, the dried form of which have to be soaked before use for about 15 minutes. They add a unique flavour to salads, fish and meat dishes, grills, soups and terrines.

Shirataki noodles
These are translucent, jelly-like noodles made out of shredded konnyaku, which is made from the starch of a potato-like plant called konnyaku imo. Shirataki noodles are formed from konnyaku blocks, and are widely used in one-pot dishes and Sukiyaki.

Soba noodles
These are made from buckwheat flour, and are boiled for use in noodle dishes accompanied by soy sauce broth, finely chopped spring onions and wasabi. Also used in salads.

Soy sauce (shoyu)
This is the most widely used liquid seasoning in Japanese cookery. Naturally fermented from soybeans and wheat, it has a rich, complex flavour, and is useful in a wide range of dishes, including rice and noodle dishes, fish and meat dishes, marinades, sauces, dressings, terrines and soups.

Star anise
This spice is used in marinades, sauces and meat dishes.

Sukiyaki sauce
A soy sauce-based seasoning which has added sugar and rice wine. It can be bought in bottled form.

Teriyaki sauce
This is a mixture of naturally brewed soy sauce, wine, vinegar, spices and sugar, and is used for barbecued and grilled dishes (such as Teriyaki and Yakitori), and as a marinade, baste or seasoning for meat, poultry and fish.

Tofu
This is processed from soybeans. As it has little taste of its own, it takes on the flavour of almost anything it is mixed with, or in which it is marinated, and adds an interesting texture and plenty of protein. It is used widely, especially in vegetarian dishes. Thin, deep-fried tofu (abura-age) is used in boiled dishes, miso soup, and rice and noodle dishes.

Udon noodles
These are thick, Japanese-style wheat noodles, usually eaten with a soy sauce-based broth, accompanied by condiments such as finely chopped spring onions or a hot pepper-based spice mixture called shichimi togarashi.

Wakame seaweed
Somewhat similar to laver (nori), this is used in salads, boiled dishes, soups, vinegared dishes and fish dishes. It should be rinsed, then soaked in water before use.

Warishita stock
This is used in cooking Sukiyaki and consists of soy sauce, sugar and rice wine. Kikkoman Sukiyaki sauce can be purchased ready made-up in bottles.

Wasabi powder
This is dissolved in water to form a paste which yields a pungent hot condiment for use with Sushi, Sashimi and dressed dishes (aemono). Wasabi is green, and is stronger than the European white horseradish.

11

SOUPS AND SAUCES

SHIITAKE MUSHROOM CONSOMMÉ

Serves 8
Preparation time: 1 hour
Cooking time: 50 minutes

2 tablespoons soya oil
1 onion, chopped finely
400 g (13 oz) minced chicken leg,
chilled
50 g (2 oz) minced onion, chilled
50 g (2 oz) minced leek, chilled
50 g (2 oz) minced carrot, chilled
1 garlic clove
30 g (1 1/4 oz) dried shiitake
mushrooms
2 dried lemon grass stalks
1 sprig of thyme
star anise
1 sprig of tarragon
10 white peppercorns
1 egg white
2 litres (3 pints) chicken stock or water
a pinch of salt
gold leaf (optional), chopped chives,
and fresh shiitake mushrooms, to
garnish

1. Heat the oil in a pan, and sauté the onion until brown. Allow to cool then mix it in a large pan with the minced chicken, minced vegetables, the garlic, and the dried shiitake mushrooms.
2. Make a bouquet garni with the herbs and peppercorns and add.
3. Mix the egg white thoroughly into the mixture. Pour in the cold chicken stock or water and add a pinch of salt then stir well.
4. Place on a high heat and bring just to the boil. Stir the consommé regularly until it begins to coagulate, which will happen shortly before it boils. Turn the heat down to a slow simmer, and cook for 40–50 minutes. Do not allow the consommé to re-boil at any time.
5. Once the consommé is cooked, remove the pan from the stove, then carefully strain it. Reheat it, season, and skim off any impurities that may be present on the surface.
6. Ladle the consommé into 8 warm bowls. Garnish with a little gold leaf if you are using it.

TIP Instead of gold leaf, the consommé can be garnished with fresh shiitake mushrooms, freshly snipped chives, finely sliced vegetables or pancakes cut into small squares or triangles.

Shiitake Mushroom Consommé; Cream of Broccoli and Lemon Grass Soup (page 14); Spiced Fish Soup (page 14)

CREAM OF BROCCOLI AND LEMON GRASS SOUP

Serves 4
Suitable for vegetarians
Preparation time: 15 minutes
Cooking time: 20 minutes

1 medium-size onion
1 tablespoon butter
500–625 g (1–1¹/4 lb) broccoli stalks
1 teaspoon dried lemon grass
500 ml (18 fl oz) vegetable or chicken stock
1 tablespoon Kikkoman soy sauce
¹/4 garlic clove, crushed
¹/4 bunch of dill
a pinch of nutmeg
a pinch of Cayenne pepper
200 ml (7 fl oz) double cream
salt and freshly ground black pepper
1 tablespoon roasted almonds

1. Cut away the core from the onion and discard. Cook the onion slowly with the butter until soft, but not brown.
2. Slice the broccoli stalks (reserve the tops for another use), add to the cooked onions with the lemon grass and cook for a further 10 minutes covered with a lid. Do not allow to brown.
3. Pour in the stock, soy sauce and garlic, bring to the boil then simmer for 10 minutes. Add the dill, nutmeg and Cayenne pepper.
4. Pour the soup mixture into a blender. Blend until the mixture is smooth then add the double cream. Season with the salt and pepper.
5. Pass the soup through a fine sieve into a clean pot. Reheat. Pour into 4 warm bowls. Garnish with roasted almonds.

SPICED FISH SOUP

Serves 4
Preparation time: 15 minutes
Cooking time: 20 minutes

500 g (1 lb) cod fillet, skinned and boned
90 ml (3 fl oz) plus 2 tablespoons Kikkoman soy sauce
¹/4 teaspoon chilli powder
¹/4 teaspoon cumin
50 g (2 oz) butter
2 medium-size onions, sliced finely
1 small leek, sliced finely
1 bulb of fennel, sliced finely
1 tablespoon mirin
190 ml (6¹/2 fl oz) fish stock or water
100 g (3¹/2 oz) oyster mushrooms
1 tablespoon fresh coriander, chopped

1. Cut the fish into walnut-size pieces and mix with the 2 tablespoons of soy sauce, the chilli powder and the cumin. Marinate for 10 minutes.
2. Heat the butter in a saucepan. Sauté the drained pieces of fish until just cooked. Remove from the pan with a slotted spoon. Add the onions, leek and fennel. Cook until soft but not brown, for about 5 minutes, then add the remaining soy sauce, mirin, and fish stock or water.
3. Cook for a further 5 minutes then add the oyster mushrooms, coriander and cooked fish pieces. Reheat to serve.

CHILLED AVOCADO AND CHILLI SOUP WITH NACHOS

Serves 4
Suitable for vegetarians
Preparation time: 15 minutes

2 ripe avocados
100 g (3¹/2 oz) soured cream
350 ml (12 fl oz) vegetable or chicken stock
¹/2 garlic clove, crushed
¹/2 tablespoon lemon juice
1 tablespoon Kikkoman soy sauce
1 – 2 teaspoons hot chilli sauce
a pinch of nutmeg
1 tablespoon shallots, diced finely
a pinch of chilli powder
2 bags of nachos (corn chips)
1 tablespoon chopped mint
1 tablespoon soured cream
a pinch of salt
freshly ground black pepper

1. Cut the avocados in half, and remove the stones and the tough outer skins. Dice the avocado flesh then place in a food processor along with all the other ingredients except the nachos and mint. Blend until smooth.
2. Pour the soup into a fine sieve and push it through with a ladle in order to strain it.
3. Pour into 4 chilled bowls and add 2 ice cubes to each bowl. Sprinkle with the chopped mint, and add the soured cream. Serve with nachos.

TIP Should the soup be a little thin or thick, simply lessen or increase the amount of vegetable stock.

TURNIP AND MISO SOUP

Serves 4
Preparation time: 20 minutes
Cooking time: 20 minutes

4 white turnips, or 12 baby turnips
2 teaspoons pickled ginger, diced finely
¹/2 lemon
1 tablespoon sliced spring onions
Broth
3 tablespoons white miso
600 ml (1 pint) dashi 1 (page 20)
2 teaspoons sugar
3 tablespoons mirin
1 tablespoon Kikkoman soy sauce
2 egg yolks

Miso is now available from almost any health food shop. These shops are sometimes full of new and interesting ingredients. Have a look, and a taste if it's allowed. It can be most inspiring.
1. Peel the thick outer skin off the turnips, then slice off the greens and scoop out the inside of the turnip so that a bowl is made. Steam the lids and turnip bowls until just cooked.
2. Grate the scooped out pieces of turnip, mix with the pickled ginger and cook in a small pan over a low heat until soft.
3. Spoon back into the cooked turnips, sprinkle with the spring onions and replace the lids.
4. Dilute the miso with a little dashi, and put both into a pan with the remaining ingredients except the egg yolks. Bring to the boil, then simmer for 2 minutes. Lightly whisk the egg yolks and stir them in so that strands of yolk form as they cook.
5. Pour the soup into 4 warm bowls. Garnish with the filled turnips and serve.

LOBSTER SOUP WITH A SMALL LOBSTER PANCAKE

Serves 4
Preparation time: 15 minutes
Cooking time: 40–45 minutes

1 kg (2.2 lb) live lobster
3 tablespoons clarified butter or oil
50 g (2 oz) shallots, or a small onion, sliced
50 g (2 oz) carrots, sliced
600 ml (1 pint) fish stock
100 ml (3¹/₂ fl oz) white wine
2 tablespoons malt vinegar
30 g (1¹/₂ oz) flour
1 tablespoon tomato purée
30 g (1¹/₂ oz) brown sugar
1 bouquet garni
1 sprig of tarragon
4 egg pancakes
4 chives
2 tablespoons double cream

1. Hold the lobster belly-side down on a wooden chopping board. Take a large knife and insert the tip through the carapace (head), then bring it down to cut through the lobster. Repeat with the remaining half. The lobster is now dead, and any further movement is a reaction from the nervous system.

2. Cut away the tail halves and reserve. Remove the gravel sack from the carapace and discard. Cut the rest into smaller pieces, reserving the claws for another use.

3. In a large pan heat the clarified butter or oil over a high heat. Add the lobster shell and cover with a lid.

4. When the lobster pieces have reddened, add the shallots and carrots, and cook for 5 minutes.

5. Heat the fish stock in a separate saucepan, then add to the lobster.

6. Pour in the white wine and vinegar then simmer until reduced by half. Add the flour and stir in the tomato purée and brown sugar.

7. Add the bouquet garni and the tarragon.

8. Allow to cook slowly for 35 minutes, skimming off any impurities from the surface. Top up with water or stock if the soup reduces too much.

9. While the soup is cooking, add the lobster tails to it for 10 minutes, then remove them. Finely dice half the lobster meat, reserving the other half for another use.

10. Spoon the lobster meat onto the centre of 4 pancakes. Bring up the sides of the pancakes to make a pouch, and tie with a chive that has been dipped in hot water.

11. Pass the soup through a fine sieve into a clean saucepan. Reheat, pour in the cream, and season to taste.

12. Heat through the lobster pancakes in a microwave or warm oven, then place them in the centre of a soup bowl. Pour the soup round each pancake to serve.

Chilled Avocado and Chilli Soup with Nachos (page 15); Lobster Soup with a Small Lobster Pancake; Turnip and Miso Soup (page 15)

WATERCRESS SOUP

Serves 4
Preparing time: 15 minutes
Cooking time: 25 minutes

200 g (7 oz) lean pork loin or leg
1 teaspoon caster sugar
600 ml (1 pint) chicken stock
200 g (7 oz) watercress
2 tablespoons sunflower oil
2 slices fresh ginger, grated finely
1 egg, beaten lightly
a little Kikkoman soy sauce
salt

1. Cut half of the pork into fine matchstick-size shreds, sprinkle the caster sugar over them, and leave to rest for 15 minutes.
2. Cut the remaining pork into small pieces, and put in a pan with the chicken stock. Bring to the boil and then the skim the surface with a ladle to remove any impurities.
3. Cook on a gentle heat for 20 minutes then pass through a fine sieve into a clean bowl.
4. Clean the watercress of any yellow leaves and cut away most of the stalks.
5. Heat 1 tablespoon of the sunflower oil in a wok. Fry the shredded pork for 2 minutes then add the watercress and grated ginger. Cook for a further minute.
6. Pour in the hot stock and bring the soup to the boil for a few seconds.
7. Turn off the soup and stir in the beaten egg. Season with soy sauce and salt to taste, then serve.

MISO SOUP WITH CHICKEN, OKRA AND LEEK

Serves 4
Preparation time: 10 minutes
Cooking time: 15 minutes

80 g (3¹/4 oz) skinned chicken leg meat
80 g (3¹/4 oz) leek
80 g (3¹/4 oz) okra
800 ml (1¹/3 pints) dashi 1 (page 20)
3 tablespoons miso
2 teaspoons grated fresh ginger
2 teaspoons Kikkoman soy sauce

1. Thinly slice the chicken leg meat. Slice the washed leek into thin rounds. If using small okra leave whole, if using large then cut in 2¹/2 cm (1-inch) thick slices.
2. Bring the dashi to the boil, and add the chicken and okra.
3. Dilute the miso with a little of the hot dashi in a cup until it becomes liquid, and pour it into the soup. Add the leek and cook for one minute longer. Squeeze the ginger for its juices with your fingers.
4. Pour into warm soup bowls, season with a few drops of ginger juice and soy sauce.

TIP Miso is a health food prepared from fermented soya beans and malt. There are other varieties available made from barley or rice, each kind having a slightly different flavour and salt level. For this dish use whichever you prefer, or if it's your first time, use the soya bean flavour, as it is delicious and easily available.

LENTIL SOUP

Serves 6
Suitable for vegetarians
Preparation time: 10 minutes
Cooking time: 1 hour

175 g (6 oz) yellow lentils
2 tablespoons sunflower oil
1 garlic clove, crushed
1 medium-size onion, sliced
1 teaspoon dried lemon grass
2 teaspoons grated ginger
2 tablespoons rice vinegar
1 small bunch of coriander, tied with string
1/4 teaspoon chilli powder
3 tablespoons Kikkoman soy sauce
1.2 litres (2 pints) chicken or vegetable stock
salt and freshly ground black pepper

Lentils are rich in protein and flavour. You can use any variety of lentil for this soup: green, orange, yellow or red.

1. Wash the lentils thoroughly in cold water, then soak them overnight.
2. Heat the sunflower oil in a large pan. Add the onions and dried lemon grass. Cook until soft but not brown, then add the remaining ingredients.
3. Bring to the boil, and skim off the impurities from the surface with a ladle.
4. Gently simmer the soup for about 1 hour until the lentils are very soft. Remember to stir from time to time, to prevent the soup from sticking.
5. When the lentils are cooked, remove the coriander and discard it. Purée the remaining soup in a blender, and then pass it through a sieve into a bowl. Season with salt and pepper, and serve.

TIP Croûtons make a wonderful garnish for this soup.

AVOCADO SOUP WITH TOASTED ALMONDS

Serves 4
Suitable for vegetarians
Preparation time: 15 minutes
Cooking time: 10 minutes

1 – 2 ripe avocados
250 ml (8 fl oz) chicken or vegetable stock
200 ml (7 fl oz) double cream
a pinch of Cayenne pepper
1/4 teaspoon nutmeg
1 tablespoon Kikkoman soy sauce
1/2 tablespoon lemon juice
1/2 teaspoon hot chilli sauce
1 teaspoon caster sugar
salt and freshly ground white pepper
1 tablespoon fresh mint, chopped
40 g (1 1/2 oz) sliced almonds

1. Remove the skin and stones from the avocados. Pass the flesh through a sieve into a bowl.
2. Heat the chicken stock and double cream with the Cayenne pepper, nutmeg and soy sauce.
3. When the liquid boils, whisk in the avocado purée to thicken, season with the lemon juice, hot chilli sauce, sugar, salt, pepper and chopped mint.
4. Toast the almonds for a few minutes under the grill until golden.
5. Reheat, but do not boil the soup. Serve immediately in warm bowls, with a few toasted almonds sprinkled on top.

DASHI

Dashi 1

6 x 15 cm (6-inch) pieces of konbu
seaweed
1 litre (1.75 pints) cold water
250 g (8 oz) dried bonito flakes

Dashi is to Japanese cookery what fish and meat stocks are to French cookery. Its flavour is uniquely Japanese, and it is used in numerous dishes. This dashi should be used for fine-flavoured broths and sauces.

1. Wipe the white film off the konbu with a clean damp cloth.
2. Place the konbu in a saucepan with the water and bring it to the boil slowly.
3. Just before the water boils remove the konbu and reserve it for dashi 2.
4. Add the bonito flakes to the konbu-flavoured water. Skim off any impurities from the surface with a ladle. Then turn off the heat.
5. When the bonito flakes settle on the bottom of the saucepan, strain the dashi through a damp tea towel or muslin cloth, reserving the bonito flakes for dashi 2.

Dashi 2

6 x 15 cm (6-inch) pieces of konbu
seaweed
1 litre (1.75 pints) cold water
250 g (8 oz) dried bonito flakes

This dashi is more strongly flavoured, and therefore is best used with meats, custards, fish and miso soups.

1. Simply place all the ingredients in a clean saucepan. Slowly bring to the boil, then pass through a damp tea towel or muslin cloth into a clean saucepan.
2. Return to the heat and simmer for a further 5–10 minutes to reduce the dashi a little so that its flavour becomes a little stronger.

TIP Dashi can also be purchased from Asian food shops in powdered tea-bag or concentrated liquid form. Although these are often acceptable nothing can capture the aroma and flavour of freshly made dashi.

Vegetarian dashi is prepared in the same way except one must omit the bonito flakes and double the amount of konbu.

NOODLE DIPPING SAUCE

2 cups dashi 2 (page 20)
3 tablespoons mirin
3 tablespoons Kikkoman soy sauce
250 g (8 oz) dried bonito flakes

This is a traditional dipping sauce for soba or wheat noodles.
1. Place all the ingredients in a saucepan and slowly bring to the boil.
2. Reduce the heat to a gentle simmer and cook for 5–10 minutes.
3. Strain through a damp tea towel or muslin cloth.

TEMPURA DIPPING SAUCE

100 ml (3½ fl oz) mirin
400 ml (14 fl oz) dashi 1 (page 20)
100 ml (3½ fl oz) Kikkoman soy sauce
1 tablespoon sugar

This dipping sauce can be used whenever fish, chicken or vegetables are cooked tempura-style (battered and deep-fried).
1. Heat the mirin in a saucepan, and flame with a match or put over a gas flame to burn off the alcohol.
2. Stir in the remaining ingredients. Remove from the heat and serve warm.

VINEGAR SOY SAUCE

2 tablespoons dashi 1 (page 20)
3 tablespoons rice vinegar
1 tablespoon Kikkoman soy sauce

Suitable for vegetarians if vegetarian dashi is used

Vinegar soy sauce tastes especially good with raw fish or shellfish and it also makes a wonderful salad dressing.
1. Simply mix all the ingredients together.

LEMON SOY SAUCE

3½ tablespoons lemon juice
4½ tablespoons Kikkoman soy sauce

Suitable for vegetarians

To prepare this sauce the Japanese use a lemon called yuzu. These are usually unobtainable outside Japan so simply use an ordinary fresh lemon instead.
1. Mix all ingredients together and serve with oysters, prawns and chicken.

TOSA SOY SAUCE

200 ml (7 fl oz) Kikkoman soy sauce
175 g (6 oz) dried bonito flakes
1 1/2 tablespoons mirin
1 tablespoon saké

Tosa soy sauce is a good dipping sauce for Sushi and Sashimi (pages 23–27).
1. Place all the ingredients in a saucepan and slowly bring to the boil. Then reduce the heat to a simmer.
2. Cook for 10 minutes then strain through a damp tea towel or muslin cloth. Allow to cool.

DIPPING SAUCE FOR COLD MEAT

2 tablespoons tahini
1 tablespoon light miso
1 tablespoon Kikkoman soy sauce
2 teaspoons caster sugar
3 tablespoons mineral water, sparkling
or still

Mix all the ingredients well together.

PLUM VINEGAR

2 umeboshi plums
1 small piece of konbu seaweed
150 ml (1/4 pint) mirin
100 ml (3 1/4 fl oz) saké
3 tablespoons rice vinegar
1 teaspoon Kikkoman light soy sauce
300 g (10 oz) dried bonito flakes

Plum vinegar is considered to be amongst the finest of all Japanese sauces. It is often served with raw shellfish. Umeboshi plums are pickled Japanese plums which you can buy bottled from an Asian food shop.
1. Place all the ingredients in a small saucepan. Bring to a gentle boil, then turn off and leave to rest for 15–20 minutes.
2. Pour the cooled plum vinegar into a clean bowl.

COLD FIRST COURSES

SUSHI

In Europe, Sushi is the single most popular Japanese food. Like so many Japanese dishes, it is very easy to make and is wonderfully nutritious; ideal for the health conscious.

Sushi is usually cooked and cooled short-grain white rice flavoured with a vinegar mixture, which is then prepared with various other ingredients, for example fish, shellfish, nori, egg pancakes, vegetables, pickled ginger and wasabi. Eventually they are presented as a Japanese-style hors d'oeuvre.

An interesting comparison between Sushi and provincial French cooking is that the ingredients other than rice used to prepare Sushi differ in Japan from region to region, much the same way as they do in France. Thus it leaves much room for variation and experimentation.

Apart from the hand-formed Sushi (Nigiri-Zushi) and rolled Sushi (Maki-Zushi) there are other varieties of Sushi, some of them are even served hot, the main ones being:

Bo-Zushi rice formed into a bar and topped with flavoured fish.
Sugata-Zushi rice topped with pre-flavoured fish such as sweetfish, in such a way as to maintain the shape of the fish.
Chirashi-Zushi rice to which flavoured vegetables are added; fish and shellfish are sometimes included.
Mushi-Zushi which is Chirashi-Zushi, steamed and served hot.
Inari-Zushi thin deep-fried tofu (abura-age), which is then boiled in a sweet sauce and stuffed with sushi rice.
Chakin-Zushi precooked and flavoured vegetables, such as shiitake mushrooms, and flaked fish are mixed with sushi rice which is then wrapped in a thin Japanese egg pancake.

SUSHI

Sushi; Sashimi (page 26)

The Sushi shown in the photograph are hand-formed Sushi (Nigiri-Zushi) and rolled Sushi (Maki-Zushi). Working from left to right and top to bottom, the Sushi in the photograph are made as follows:

1. Hand-carve carrots and spring onions and arrange with wasabi to make lovely decorations. However for a more modest display, a small ball or leaf of wasabi horseradish on your chosen serving plate will suffice.

2. Hand-roll vinegared rice and top with slices of tuna fish and a band of nori seaweed.

3. Hand-roll vinegared rice topped with a smear of wasabi and pieces of squid. Make the chess-board effect on the squid by slicing 3 cm (1 1/4-inch) squares of squid three-quarters of the way through the squid, first lengthways then across.

4. Hand-roll vinegared rice and top with a smear of wasabi and thin slices of scallop and scallop roe.

5. Hand-mould some vinegared rice into a tear-drop shape. Roll the rice log in a half sheet of nori seaweed, then roll in a bamboo mat or cling film which will help the nori adhere to the rice, and the rice log to keep its shape. Rest the log for 10 minutes then unwrap and cut into 2–3 cm (3/4–1 1/4-inch) slices. Top with salmon eggs.

6. Divide equal quantities of vinegared rice into three bowls. Mix a teaspoon of light miso into one bowl and a teaspoon of dark miso into another. Mould the rice from the three bowls into small tear-drop shapes and wrap each in a half sheet of nori seaweed. Put them at one end of a bamboo mat or sheet of plastic film, and roll tightly. Rest the log for 10 minutes before unwrapping. Slice into 2 cm (3/4-inch) slices.

7. Place a sheet of nori seaweed on a bamboo mat or a sheet of cling film. Spoon a trail of vinegared rice along one edge of the nori, leaving a 5 cm (2-inch) band clear. Top the rice with cooked king prawns, then spoon another trail of rice on top of the prawns. Fold the nori over the rice and prawns. Using a bamboo mat or cling film, roll up the rice, prawns and nori as if making a swiss roll. Leave to rest for 10 minutes before unwrapping and slicing into 2 cm (3/4-inch) pieces. Garnish

each slice with a teaspoon of pickled vegetables.

8. Hand-roll vinegared rice, smear with wasabi and top with sliced swordfish, egg pancake and red pepper.

9. As condiments, try the Tosa Soy Sauce (page 22) and grated daikon rolled into a ball.

TIP When preparing Sushi simply make as much or as little as you need. Always serve it as soon as possible. Many Japanese food shops sell the fish pre-sliced ready for preparing Sushi. Many will also sell ready-made Sushi.

MAKI-ZUSHI

Serves 8
Preparation time: 20 minutes, plus cooling of rice
Cooking time: 30 minutes

300 g (10 oz) short-grain rice
8 cm (3-inch) piece of konbu seaweed
1 tablespoon saké or dry white wine
400 g (13 oz) salmon fillet, skinned
1 cucumber, peeled
1 small jar of salmon roe
2 teaspoons pickled ginger
5–6 sheets of nori
1 thin wooden mat for rolling nori, or a tea towel
salt and freshly ground black pepper
Vinegar seasoning
2¹/₂ tablespoons rice vinegar
1 tablespoon caster sugar
1 teaspoon salt
Condiments
wasabi
Kikkoman soy sauce, for dipping

1. Wash the rice in cold running water until clear. Place in a pan with 350 ml (12 fl oz) of cold water, the konbu and saké. Cover with a tight-fitting lid and bring to the boil.

2. Remove the konbu and replace the lid. Turn to a low heat for 15 minutes then switch off the heat and allow the rice to steam for a further 10–15 minutes.

3. Using a wooden spoon, carefully mix the rice to make it fluffy then replace the lid. When the rice is fully cooked, transfer it to a shallow bowl.

4. Gently and quickly mix in the vinegar seasoning, allow to cool a little, then cover with a damp tea towel to prevent the rice from drying out.

5. Cut the salmon and cucumber into long thin strips.

6. Lay the nori out flat on the thin wooden mat or on a dry tea towel.

7. Leaving 5 cm (2 inches) of nori clear, spoon a thin line of sushi rice across the width of the nori, then lay on a line of salmon, cucumber, pickled ginger and salmon roe. Top with some more sushi rice.

8. Fold over the end of the nori, then, using the wooden mat or tea towel, roll the nori and its filling as for a swiss roll.

9. Leave rolled up for 10 minutes so that the moisture of the filling seeps into the nori which in turn act as a mould once the wooden mat or tea towel is removed.

10. After 10 minutes unroll the mat or tea towel, and cut the Sushi into 3 cm (1¹/4-inch) lengths. Present as in the photograph with the condiments.

SASHIMI

Sashimi is something many people like to enjoy both in restaurants and at home these days. When a traditional dish like Sashimi is served, it is best to keep it as authentic as possible. There is nothing complicated about Sashimi, as you will realise from the following tips.

Almost any fish can be used for Sashimi. The two important things to remember are:

1. Use only the freshest seasonal fish.

2. Use fish that are suitable to be eaten raw, such as tuna, kingfish, saltwater salmon, mackerel, sea bream, squid, halibut, Seychelle's fish and scallops.

Two other points to remember are the presentation and the condiments. Presentation should always be clean and aesthetically pleasing to the eye. Lay the fish on the serving platter in as artistic a way as possible. I have presented Sashimi in circles like flower petals, as the wing of a bird in flight, or simply in neat rows that show the colours of the fish. The condiments are often hot and help flavour the Sashimi; more importantly, they aid digestion of the raw fish.

Soy sauce is almost indispensable with whatever kind of Sashimi is served. Daikon (Japanese white radish), seaweed (such as nori), grated ginger, wasabi (Japanese green horseradish paste), and spring onions are all excellent condiments to serve with Sashimi, served separately in small bowls.

Sashimi, like Sushi, involves the preparation of raw fish, and is at the heart of Japanese cuisine. It does not involve any cooking so it is quick and easy to prepare and retains its full nutritional value. When buying fish for Sashimi, look for freshness and quality. Here are some tips:

1. Smell the fish: it should smell of the sea. Any strong fishy odour indicates that the fish is more than a day old.

2. If the skin of the fish is sticky and slimy, this means it is not fresh. The fish flesh should be firm to the touch.

3. The eyes of the fish should always be plump and clear, never sunken and dull.

4. Fish gills become dark and pungent with age; fresh fish have gills that are pink to red and are almost odourless.

Other seafoods that make wonderful Sashimi are squid, lobster, turbot and abalone. Again, remember that freshness is most important; if possible, all shellfish should be kept live until needed.

The thought of eating raw fish may seem strange, yet many Westerners who have either visited Japan, or having dined in a Japanese restaurant soon learn to appreciate and enjoy this unique food: it has simple uncomplicated flavours and a texture unlike anything else.

The Sashimi in the photograph was sliced from skinned and boned fillets of fish bought from my fishmonger. Buying the fish ready-filleted makes the preparation quicker and simpler. Find a fishmonger who is familiar with Japanese dishes if possible, otherwise tell your fishmonger you are making Sashimi, so he will choose his freshest fish.

In the photograph on page 24, the small rose consists of pickled ginger with wasabi leaves, then there is a ball of grated fresh ginger, and a carved carrot junk with soy sauce; the inner floret of the fish flower is tuna fish, the outer is swordfish, and in the middle is scallop.

1. Wash the fish and scallops in plenty of ice cold water. Dry with a clean cloth.
2. Slice the fresh fish and scallops, and arrange on a Japanese tray or serving plate in an attractive way. I have chosen to make a rose, by rolling one piece of fish then adding a number of slices, one after the other, as if putting petals onto a flower. The same method is used with the sliced pickled ginger.
3. Pour some Tosa Soy Sauce (page 22) into a small bowl. If you are feeling adventurous, carve a bowl from a carrot, then pour in the dipping sauce.
4. Peel 5 cm (2 inches) fresh ginger with a small knife. Grate it, then roll into a ball after squeezing out a little juice.
5. Display the Sashimi and condiments as in the photograph or in a simpler way, whichever you prefer. Serve immediately.

TIP Make as much or as little Sashimi as you like; there is no set recipe. It is the method of preparation and serving that is most important.

GRILLED SEA URCHIN

Serves 4
Preparation time: 15 minutes
Cooking time: 6 minutes

200 g (7 oz) cooked crabmeat
1 egg white, beaten lightly

^{1}/4 teaspoon salt
^{1}/2 teaspoon saké
^{1}/2 teaspoon mirin or dry white wine
1 tub of fresh sea urchin roe
1 egg yolk
black poppy seeds
Kikkoman soy sauce, to dip

Unfortunately sea urchins are not seen on many tables, so just for a change why not try this recipe. It's delightful!

1. Tear the crabmeat by hand into small pieces and place in a bowl with the egg white, salt, saké and mirin. Mix all the ingredients together.

2. Pour the mixture into a 500 g (1 lb) greased cake or loaf baking tin. Wet your hand and smooth out the mixture so that it is around 2–3 cm (^{3}/4–1^1/4 inch) deep, and level on top.

3. Cover the crabmeat with the sea urchin roe, and brush with the egg yolk. Brush several times, as this will give the finished dish an appetising glaze.

4. Place the baking tin on a grill rack 13–16 cm (5–6 inches) below the grill. Grill for 5 minutes until cooked. Remove and sprinkle on the poppy seeds, and return to the grill for 30 seconds. This will bring out the flavour of the poppy seeds.

5. Remove from the grill, and allow to cool completely. Slice into squares or triangles, or cut into rounds with a cutter, or simply slice as a terrine. Serve by itself as an hors d'oeuvre, or with salad for a main meal, using the soy sauce as a dipping sauce.

Grilled Sea Urchin

RUBY GRAPEFRUIT WITH SAKÉ, BLACK PEPPER AND MINT

Serves 4
Suitable for vegetarians
Preparation time: 15 minutes

4 ruby grapefruit, chilled
8 fresh mint leaves
4 nips of chilled saké
freshly ground black pepper
raspberries and mint sprigs, to garnish

This dish is so easy to prepare and has a wonderfully refreshing flavour.

1. Using a sharp knife, remove the outer skin from the grapefruits, then cut the segments out into a chilled bowl.
2. Finely slice the leaves of mint and mix through the grapefruit. Spoon the mixture into chilled champagne glasses or something similar.
3. Pour a little saké into each glass, and grind a little black pepper into each glass. Garnish with a few raspberries and mint.

Ruby Grapefruit with Saké, Black Pepper and Mint

MELON WITH PARMA HAM AND PASSION-FRUIT VINAIGRETTE

Serves 4
Preparation time: 15 minutes

1 ogen melon (or whichever is seasonal)
8 slices of Parma ham
Dressing
pulp of 1 passion-fruit
1–1¹/2 tablespoons white wine vinegar
2 tablespoons sunflower oil
2 teaspoons walnut oil
a pinch of sugar
¹/2 teaspoon mild mustard
a pinch of salt

1. Cut the melon in half and spoon out the seeds. Using a melon baller, make as many melon balls as the melon will allow.
2. Place all the dressing ingredients in a sealable jar and shake for 10 seconds to mix the dressing.
3. To serve, place equal quantities of melon balls on each plate, top each with two thin slices of Parma ham, rolled or curled. Finally, dress each with a little passion-fruit dressing.

AVOCADO WITH GINGER DRESSING

Serves 2
Suitable for vegetarians
Preparation time: 10 minutes

1 ripe avocado
Dressing
¹/2 teaspoon grated fresh ginger
3 tablespoons sunflower oil
1 tablespoon lemon juice
a pinch of brown sugar
a pinch of salt and pepper

Try this when you are in a hurry.
1. Cut the avocado in half and remove the stone. Cut a thin line lengthways through the skin of each half. This will now allow you to peel off the skin leaving the flesh intact.
2. Mix the dressing ingredients together and whisk with a fork or place in a sealable jar. Shake the jar to mix the dressing.
3. Place the avocado halves in small bowls, pour over a little dressing and serve.

MELON AND PRAWNS WITH SWEET AND SOUR SAUCE

Serves 4
Preparation time: 20 minutes

1 melon (whichever kind is seasonal and ripe)
12 king prawns
4 mint sprigs
Sweet and sour sauce
2 tablespoons malt vinegar
30 g (1¼ oz) brown sugar
5 tablespoons canned or carton pineapple juice
3 tablespoons tomato juice
½ teaspoon grated fresh ginger
½ garlic clove, crushed
2 teaspoons Kikkoman soy sauce
1 teaspoon gelatine, soaked in a little water
½ teaspoon hot chilli sauce
a pinch of salt

The prawns are easily bought cooked and frozen which reduces the preparation time.

1. Cut the melon in half, discard the seeds and cut away the tough outer skin. Using a melon baller, scoop melon balls from one half of the melon.
2. Cut the remaining half in half again, then finely slice it.
3. Place the vinegar and sugar in a small pan and reduce by half on a high heat.
4. Add the pineapple juice and tomato juice, with the ginger, garlic and soy sauce. Heat until the sauce simmers.
5. Add the soaked gelatine and remove from the heat. Pass through a fine sieve and season with salt and hot chilli sauce. Allow the sauce to cool.
6. Place the sliced melon in the centre of 4 plates. Top each with 3 prawns, garnish with the melon balls and mint sprigs. Pour a little of the chilled sweet and sour sauce over each dish to serve.

PRAWN AND TOFU PÂTÉ

Serves 6
Preparation time: 20 minutes
Cooking time: 50 minutes

500 g (1 lb) pike fillet, skinned and boned
250 g (8 oz) soft tofu
2 large eggs (size 2)
1 tablespoon tomato purée
2 teaspoons ginger juice (page 39)
1 tablespoon Kikkoman soy sauce
20 g (¾ oz) chopped fresh parsley
75 g (3 oz) sliced spring onions
12 king prawn tails, de-veined

Preheat the oven to Gas Mark 2/150°C/300°F.

1. Place the pike, tofu, eggs, tomato purée, ginger and soy sauce in a food processor. Blend until smooth. Then fold through the chopped parsley and sliced spring onions.
2. Grease a terrine or meatloaf tin and line it with cling film. Pour half the fish mixture into the mould. Lay the prawn tails tail to tail along the mould, and pour the remaining fish mixture into it.
3. Cover with buttered foil or a lid. Place in a hot waterbath and cook in the oven until firm to the touch, about 50 minutes.
4. Remove from the waterbath. Cool and refrigerate the paté overnight.
5. Slice when chilled and serve with crisp lettuce.

TIP Another excellent accompaniment for this is a two-to-one mixture of mayonnaise and horseradish sauce.

TEA-SMOKED DUCK WITH PINEAPPLE AND PEPPERCORN DRESSING

Serves 4
Preparation time: 10–15 minutes
Cooking time: 30 minutes

2 large cleaned duck breasts
1 tablespoon Kikkoman soy sauce
1 small pineapple
20 g (3/4 oz) clarified butter
1 head of frisée lettuce
Peppercorn dressing
1 dessertspoon green peppercorns
1/2 teaspoon Dijon mustard
2 dessertspoons hazelnut oil
2 tablespoons olive oil
2 dessertspoons white wine vinegar
salt and freshly ground black pepper
Smoking mixture
1 cup Chinese tea
1 cup rice
1 cup brown sugar

1. Score the fatty skin of each duck breast with a sharp knife, so the fat can cook and render down whilst smoking. Then brush each breast with soy sauce.

2. Mix the smoking mixture together, and place it in the bottom of a small foil-lined steamer or wok. Lay the duck breast on a steaming tray, at least 2–3 inches above the smoking mixture. Cover with a tight sealing lid and damp tea towels. Place on a high heat for 6–8 minutes then on a low heat for 15–18 minutes.

3. Take the whole pot or wok outside and remove the lid. Remove the duck breasts and bring back inside the kitchen to cool.

4. Remove the thick outside skin of the pineapple with a sharp knife. Slice finely into 12 slices. Reserve any leftover pineapple for fruit salad or some other dessert.

5. In a large hot frying pan, place a little clarified butter, sauté each slice of pineapple quickly, making sure that each side is lightly coloured. When all the pineapple slices are cooked, cut each in half.

6. Mix all the dressing ingredients together in a sealable jar.

7. To serve, place six halves of pineapples in a circle in the centre of each plate. Top each with lettuce and a few thin slices of duck breast. Pour a little peppercorn dressing over each. Serve cold.

TIP This dish can be prepared well in advance of any planned meal. If there is any duck breast left over, cover with cling film and refrigerate, as it will easily keep for up to a week.

Tea-smoked Duck with Pineapple and Peppercorn Dressing; Prawn and Tofu Pâté (page 31); Melon and Prawns with Sweet and Sour Sauce (page 31)

FRESH TUNA FISH MARINATED WITH MIXED HERBS AND TOMATOES

Serves 4
Preparation time: 20 minutes, plus marinating time

1 tomato
400 g (13 oz) tuna fish fillets
30 g (1¹/₄ oz) spring onion, sliced finely
1 tablespoon fresh tarragon, chopped
1 tablespoon grated or bottled horseradish
1 teaspoon sesame oil
juice from 2 lemons

This lovely dish is a sort of European Sashimi. It's so quick and easy. Be sure that the fish you buy is absolutely fresh.

1. To make tomato concassé, remove the stalk from the tomato and prick the top with a knife. Plunge into boiling water for 10 seconds and then immediately into ice cold water. Remove the skin by carefully peeling it away from the tomato. Then cut it into quarters, spoon out the seeds, and discard them. Dice the remaining tomato flesh.

2. Cut the tuna fish into finger-length slices.

3. Place all the ingredients into a bowl and mix well. Refrigerate for 4 hours, re-mixing every hour. Serve chilled on its own or with crisp lettuce.

SARDINE HORS D'OEUVRE SPREAD

Serves 4
Preparation time: 10 minutes

250 g (8 oz) canned sardines
250 g (8 oz) cream cheese
1 tablespoon Kikkoman soy sauce
1 teaspoon lemon juice
1 teaspoon horseradish sauce
3 tablespoons chopped fresh parsley
a pinch of Cayenne pepper
a pinch of salt

1. Remove the bones from the sardines. Place the sardines in a food processor and blend with the remaining ingredients. Push the mixture through a sieve to remove any bones. Chill for 1 hour before use.

TERRINE OF CHICKEN WITH PICKLED GINGER AND SAKÉ

Serves 6
Preparation time: 15 minutes
Cooking time: 45 minutes

450 g (15 oz) chicken fillets or breast,
cut into fingers
a little white wine
1 garlic clove, crushed
a little fresh ginger, grated
a little fresh thyme, chopped
a little fresh coriander, chopped
10 leek leaves
butter for greasing
1/2 bulb garlic cloves
300 ml (1/2 pint) saké
3 1/2 tablespoons Kikkoman soy sauce
1 1/2 tablespoons honey
8 leaves gelatine, soaked (or 16 g
powdered, soaked)
salt and freshly ground black pepper

1. Marinate the chicken overnight in white wine, garlic, ginger, thyme and coriander. Drain when ready to use.
2. Blanch the leek leaves by immersing in boiling water for 2 minutes. Line a small buttered terrine mould with lengths of blanched leek, overlapping the sides too.
3. Roast the garlic cloves in the oven at Gas Mark 4/180°/350°F for 3–4 minutes, or under the grill for 2 minutes. Reset the oven to Gas Mark 2/150°C/300°F.
4. Layer the fillets or fingers of chicken in the terrine mould with the pickled ginger and the garlic until nearly full.
5. Heat the saké, soy sauce and honey in a saucepan. When hot add the soaked gelatine and allow it to dissolve. Season the saké with salt and pepper.
6. Pour the saké mixture into the terrine mould. Allow the saké just to cover the chicken. Fold the overlapped leek leaves over the chicken. Cover with a lid.
7. Place in a hot water-bath (bain marie) and cook for 30–45 minutes.
8. When cooked allow to cool. Refrigerate for 5–6 hours until the saké has set. Turn out of the terrine and slice.

TIP This terrine has a wonderful combination of flavours and looks beautiful. Serve it when you feel like something light and a little different.

SMOKED MUSSEL PATÉ

Serves 4–6
Preparation time: 10 minutes

150 g (5 oz) smoked mussels, fresh or
canned
150 g (5 oz) soured cream
100 g (3 1/2 oz) cream cheese
2 teaspoons Dijon mustard
1 tablespoon lemon juice
1 tablespoon Kikkoman soy sauce
1 tablespoon chopped chives

1. If using canned mussels, drain away the oil. Place in a food processor with all the other ingredients except the chopped chives. Blend until smooth. Chill for 1 hour.
2. Sprinkle with chopped chives to serve.

TROUT MARINATED WITH LIME, BLACK PEPPER AND FRESH CORIANDER

Serves 4
Preparation time: 20 minutes plus marinating

Ginger vinaigrette
1 tablespoon sliced ginger
5 tablespoons sunflower oil
2 tablespoons rice vinegar
1 teaspoon honey
a few stalks of coriander
Trout marinade
500 g (1 lb) side of fresh trout, or 2 smaller sides
1 tablespoon crushed black peppercorns
1 tablespoon lime zest
1 tablespoon chopped fresh coriander
200 g (7 oz) rock salt
125 g (4 oz) brown sugar
a mixture of lettuce and coriander leaves
1/2 teaspoon poppy seeds
1 tablespoon toasted sesame seeds
4 lime segments

Make sure the fish you buy is absolutely fresh.

1. Prepare the ginger vinaigrette by simply placing all the ingredients in a sealable bottle or container, shaking well for 30 seconds then allowing the flavours to infuse for at least 1 hour. Shake once more before serving.

2. Lay the side of trout on a chopping board, and using a potato peeler, pull out the fine vein of bones that runs from the head toward the tail. Then place in a shallow tray. Sprinkle over the crushed black peppercorns, lime zest and coriander.

3. Finally mix together the rock salt and brown sugar. Sprinkle this over the trout fillet. Cover with cling film. Refrigerate overnight, then wash off the salt mixture early the next morning.

4. Slice the trout into fine slices using a sharp carving knife. Trout prepared this way will keep easily for 1 week under refrigeration.

5. Present the dish by laying the lettuce and coriander leaves in the centre of 4 plates, laying the sliced trout over the lettuce, and pouring a little ginger vinaigrette around the trout. Sprinkle the poppy seeds and toasted sesame seeds on the vinaigrette. Garnish with the lime segments and a few leaves of fresh coriander to serve.

TIP This style of marinating preserves the fish and can be used with other fish or shellfish just as easily, e.g. salmon, turbot and scallops.

HOT FIRST COURSES

GRILLED AUBERGINE WITH PEANUT SAUCE

Serves 4
Suitable for vegetarians
Preparation time: 15 minutes
Cooking time: 15 minutes

1 large aubergine
3 tablespoons olive oil
salt and freshly ground black pepper

Peanut sauce
1 garlic clove, crushed
150 ml (1/4 pint) warm water
5 tablespoons smooth peanut butter
2 tablespoons Kikkoman soy sauce
hot chilli sauce to taste
1 teaspoon grated ginger
1/4 teaspoon Cayenne pepper

1. Cut the aubergine into slices around 1 cm (1/2 inch) thick. Lay them on a grilling tray. Brush each with olive oil and season with the salt and pepper. Grill the aubergine on both sides until cooked.
2. Prepare the peanut sauce by placing all the ingredients in a small pan. Bring to the boil slowly and cook for 2 minutes.
3. To serve, top each grilled piece of aubergine with a little peanut sauce.

Grilled Aubergine with Peanut Sauce

CHICKEN LIVERS WITH SPINACH AND POPPY SEEDS

Serves 4
Preparation time: 15 minutes
Cooking time: 10 minutes

250 g (8 oz) chicken livers
2 tablespoons sunflower oil
300 g (10 oz) spinach
2 spring onions, sliced finely
1 teaspoon poppy seeds
Sauce
2 tablespoons Kikkoman soy sauce
2 tablespoons mirin or dry sherry
2 tablespoons mineral water, sparkling or still
1 tablespoon caster sugar

1. Cut away any sinew from the chicken livers.
2. Heat 1 tablespoon of the oil in a wok or large frying pan, add the spinach and spring onions, and stir-fry until the spinach becomes dark in colour and tender.
3. Transfer to a serving bowl or plate. Wipe dry the wok or frying pan with paper towels.
4. Heat the remaining tablespoon of oil in the wok or frying pan and stir-fry the chicken livers for 3 minutes.
5. Pour in all the sauce ingredients, and cook for a further 3 minutes.
6. Spoon the cooked chicken livers and sauce onto the spinach. Garnish with poppy seeds and serve.

TIP You may of course serve the spinach and chicken livers in 4 smaller bowls.

LEEK AND WHITEBAIT FRITTERS

Serves 4
Preparation time: 15 minutes
Cooking time 10–15 minutes

1 small leek
100 ml (3½ fl oz) tempura batter (page 78)
100 g (3½ oz) whitebait
100 ml (3½ fl oz) sunflower oil
1 lime cut into wedges
fresh coriander to garnish
Dipping sauce
3 tablespoons Kikkoman soy sauce
1½ teaspoons hot chilli sauce
100 ml (3½ fl oz) dashi 2 (page 20)
1 teaspoon sesame oil
2 teaspoons caster sugar

1. Mix all the dipping sauce ingredients together in a small bowl and stir until the sugar dissolves. Pour into 4 small serving bowls.
2. Slice the leek very finely. Place in a colander and wash under cold running water, then drain.
3. Mix together the tempura batter, leek and the whitebait in a large bowl.
4. Heat the sunflower oil in a large frying pan. Drop 1 tablespoon amounts of the whitebait mixture into the oil, taking care to leave space between each fritter. When golden, turn over and cook the other side. Repeat until all the mixture is used.
5. Divide the fritters into equal amounts. Serve on 4 plates, garnished with lime wedges and fresh coriander, and accompanied by the dipping sauce.

SMALL PEA AND HAM PUDDINGS

Serves 4
Preparation time: 20 minutes
Cooking time: 20 minutes

2 tablespoons sunflower oil
100 g (3½ oz) white bread cubes
400 g (13 oz) cooked green peas
a small pinch of Cayenne pepper
2 eggs
100 ml (3½ fl oz) whipping cream
½ tablespoon Dijon mustard
25 g (1 oz) diced ham
butter for greasing
salt and freshly ground black pepper
Sauce
100 g (3½ oz) azuki beans (soaked in cold water overnight)
1 tablespoon salt and freshly ground black pepper
300 ml (½ pint) dashi 1 (page 20)
2 teaspoons mirin
1 tablespoon Kikkoman soy sauce
1 teaspoon ginger juice (see below)
1 sprig of fresh rosemary, bruised
1 garlic clove, crushed
a little diluted arrowroot or cornflour

1. Preheat the oven to Gas Mark 3/160°C/325°F.
2. Make the croûtons by heating the oil in a frying pan and frying the white bread cubes until golden.
3. Place the peas, Cayenne and eggs in a food processor, and blend until smooth. Add the cream, and blend once more. Pour the mixture into a bowl. Fold in with a spatula the fried croûtons, mustard and ham. Season to taste. Pour into 4 buttered timbales or cups. Cover each with butter paper or tin foil.
4. Poach in a water-bath in the oven for 15–20 minutes until firm to the touch. Rest before turning out.
5. Place the azuki beans in seasoned cold water. Bring to the boil, then simmer for 30 minutes until soft. Drain and keep warm.
6. Heat the dashi with the mirin, soy sauce, ginger juice, rosemary and garlic. Cook for 5 minutes, then pass through a fine sieve into a clean pot. Add the azuki beans and reheat once more, then thicken a little with the diluted arrowroot or cornflour.
7. Unmould the pea and ham puddings and pour a little azuki sauce around each pudding to serve.

TIP Ginger juice is obtained by finely grating some peeled fresh ginger, then squeezing it between your fingers.

WARM SALAD OF PRAWN AND CELERIAC RAVIOLI

Serves 4
Preparation time: 25 minutes
Cooking time: 15 minutes

100 g (3¹/₂ oz) mixed salad leaves and
fresh herbs (4 small handfuls)
2 tablespoons vinaigrette
1 celeriac
1 tablespoon salt
250 ml (8 fl oz) water
1 teaspoon chopped chives
1 tablespoon Kikkoman soy sauce
8 uncooked king prawns, minced
1 egg for egg wash
a pinch of flour
100 ml (3¹/₂ fl oz) corn oil
Lemon grass butter sauce
¹/₂ teaspoon grated ginger
2 teaspoons lemon juice
1 tablespoon mirin
1 teaspoon shallot, diced finely
2 stalks of lemon grass, crushed
80 g (3¹/₄ oz) unsalted butter
salt and freshly ground black pepper

This is a wonderful dish and is well worth the extra effort.

1. Toss the salad leaves with the vinaigrette.

2. Peel the tough outer skin off the celeriac. Slice 40 thin slices 1–2 mm (¹/₈-inch) thick, then cut these into rounds using a 5 cm (2-inch) pastry cutter.

3. Dissolve the salt in the water and soak the rounds until the celeriac becomes soft and pliable. Drain them, then lay them on a tea towel to dry.

4. Mix the chives, soy sauce and minced prawns together.

5. Egg wash each round of celeriac, and sprinkle with a little flour. Place a little minced prawn in the centre of 20 celeriac rounds. Cover each with the remaining celeriac rounds. Seal each with your fingers.

6. Heat the oil in a large frying pan. Sauté the celeriac ravioli a few at a time until golden on both sides.

7. Squeeze the ginger for its juice using your fingers. Heat the lemon juice, mirin, ginger juice, shallots and crushed lemon grass in a small pan and simmer until reduced by half.

8. Remove the pan from the heat and whisk in the unsalted butter in walnut-size pieces one at a time, and season. Return the pan to the heat should the sauce become cold. Pass the sauce through a fine sieve into a small warm bowl.

9. Place the salad leaves in the centre of 4 plates. Surround the leaves with 5 celeriac ravioli, pour a little lemon grass sauce over each ravioli, and serve.

Small Pea and Ham Puddings (page 39); Steamed Chicken and Prawn Custard (page 42); Warm Salad of Prawn and Celeriac Ravioli

STEAMED CHICKEN AND PRAWN CUSTARD

Serves 5
Preparation time: 20 minutes
Cooking time: 30 minutes

500 ml (18 fl oz) dashi 1 (page 20)
5 eggs (size 2–3)
a pinch of salt
1 chicken breast
2 teaspoons Kikkoman soy sauce
1 tablespoon saké or dry white wine
4 leaves of spinach
40 g (1¹/₂ oz) carrots, sliced thinly
4 shiitake mushrooms (or mushrooms of your choice)
8 king prawns

1. Gently heat the dashi until it is just warm.

2. Crack the eggs into a bowl, season with salt and beat a little with a fork. Slowly pour the dashi onto the eggs and lightly whisk. Do not over-whisk, as it will make too many bubbles.

3. Cut away the bone from the chicken breast, and slice the flesh into 4 thin slices. Leave to marinate in the soy sauce and saké or wine for 15 minutes.

4. Blanch the spinach in hot water for 10 seconds and refresh in ice cold water. Repeat with the carrots. De-stalk the mushrooms.

5. Remove the head and shell from the king prawns. Remove the vein by slightly cutting into the back of the prawns and washing out the vein in cold water.

6. Neatly arrange the chicken, mushrooms, prawns, spinach and carrots in 4 deep bowls or cups. Pour over the egg and dashi mixture. Allow the ingredients to show a little. Cover with cling film or with lids.

7. Place in a hot steamer, and replace the lid. Turn the heat down to a gentle steam for around 15–20 minutes. To test if the custards are cooked, insert a skewer. If it comes out clean they are cooked; if not, steam a little longer.

8. Serve the bowls or cups on small base plates or saucers.

HONEYED CHICKEN AND WARM MANGETOUT

Serves 4
Preparation time: 15 minutes
Cooking time: 10 minutes

12 chicken fillets or 2 chicken breasts
cut into 12 fingers
150 g (5 oz) mangetout
1 tablespoon sunflower oil
1/2 teaspoon sesame oil
1 tablespoon honey
1 tablespoon mineral water
1 tablespoon lemon juice
2 teaspoons Kikkoman soy sauce
1 teaspoon wholegrain mustard
1 tablespoon salted butter
salt and freshly ground black pepper

Next time you purchase some chicken breasts save and freeze the little fillets from the bone side of the chicken breasts. They are perfect for this dish.

1. Bring a large pan of salted water to the boil.

2. Pick the stalks off the mangetout then cook them in the boiling salted water for 1–2 minutes until just crisp. Drain them in a colander.

3. Heat the sunflower oil in a frying pan. Season the chicken fillets, then cook them in the hot oil until golden all over.

4. Drain off the oil, add the honey, water, lemon juice and soy sauce.

5. Bring the sauce to the boil, add the mustard and gently whisk in the salted butter.

6. Toss the warm mangetout with a few drops of sesame oil and a pinch of salt.

7. Place the mangetout in equal amounts in the centre of 4 warm plates. Top each with 3 chicken fillets and a little of the sauce and serve.

BURMESE KING PRAWNS WITH A ROASTED GARLIC DIPPING SAUCE

Serves 4
Preparation time: 15 minutes
Cooking time: 10 minutes

16 king prawn tails (uncooked)
1 tablespoon olive oil
salt and freshly ground black pepper

Roasted garlic sauce
6 garlic cloves
2 egg yolks
2 teaspoons chopped anchovies
2–3 tablespoons lemon juice
200 ml (7 fl oz) olive oil
4 black olives, chopped finely
1 tablespoon chopped fresh parsley
a small pinch of Cayenne pepper

1. First make the sauce. Roast the garlic cloves in their skins if your oven is already switched on, otherwise roast them under the grill for 4–5 minutes. Remove from the heat, allow to cool, then remove the skins. Crush with a fork to make a paste.

2. Place the egg yolks in a small bowl with the crushed garlic, anchovies and 1 tablespoon of the lemon juice.

3. Slowly whisk in the olive oil, pouring on only a thin thread to begin with. Gradually whisk in the remaining lemon juice and olive oil.

4. Finally add the black olives, parsley and Cayenne pepper. The sauce should be rich and creamy.

5. Shell the king prawns and, using a small knife, make a small cut along the back of each prawn. Wash out the dark coloured veins with cold water.

6. Lay the prawns on a grill tray, brush with olive oil and season with salt and pepper. Grill under a high heat on both sides until the prawns become pink in colour and firm to the touch.

7. Place the roasted garlic sauce in a small bowl, place this bowl in the centre of a large plate. Neatly arrange the prawns around the bowl. Garnish with spring onions to serve.

TIP This same dish could be prepared using small pieces of boneless chicken. Try it, as it's just as enjoyable but less expensive than prawns.

Burmese King Prawns with a Roasted Garlic Dipping Sauce

Prawn Fries; Squid with Soy Sauce (page 46)

PRAWN FRIES

Serves 4
Preparation time: 15 minutes
Cooking time: 10 minutes

8 raw king prawn tails
1/4 garlic clove, crushed
a pinch of salt
1 teaspoon lemon juice
a small pinch of Cayenne pepper
8 slices of sandwich bread
30 g (1 1/4 oz) sesame seeds
oil for deep-frying
Kikkoman soy sauce

1. Place the prawn tails, garlic, salt, lemon juice and Cayenne pepper in a food processor and mince to a fine paste.
2. Spread the prawn paste on one side of the sandwich bread. Cut off the crusts, then cut each slice into four. Sprinkle with sesame seeds.
3. Heat the oil until a cube of day-old bread turns golden in a few seconds. Deep-fry the fries in hot oil until golden. Remove from the fat and drain.
4. Serve with soy sauce to dip.

TIP If fresh prawns are used, these fries can be made in advance and frozen. When they are needed, cook from frozen.

SQUID WITH SOY SAUCE

Serves 4
Preparation time: 15 minutes
Cooking time: 15 minutes

salt
2 large squid, each weighing about
300 g (10 oz)
2 tablespoons sunflower oil
2 tablespoons caster sugar
1 tablespoon Kikkoman soy sauce
2 garlic cloves, crushed

1. Dip your fingers in the salt and pull off the purple cuticles on the outside of the squid tubes, then pull out the tentacles. Cut off the piece that comes from inside the squid and discard.
2. Wash the squid tubes and the remaining tentacles in cold running water.
3. Cut the squid tubes into rings, then the tentacles into 5 cm (2-inch) pieces.
4. Heat the oil in a saucepan, add the squid, cook for 5 minutes then add the caster sugar. Caramelise the sugar, then pour in the soy sauce and crushed garlic and any juice left on the board from cutting the squid.
5. Cook over a low heat for a further 10 minutes. Serve with rice.

GRILLED OYSTERS WITH LEMON PEPPER AND CHÈVRE

Serves 4
Preparation time: 10 minutes

4 oysters
1/4 teaspoon lemon pepper
60 g (2 1/4 oz) chèvre, plain or herbed
Decoration
rock salt
paprika

This dish makes an exciting starter to almost any meal. It is inexpensive and need not be presented as I have done. Something less visual is very acceptable, remembering that taste is always paramount.
1. Open the oysters with an oyster knife. Place under a hot grill for 30 seconds, then remove.
2. Sprinkle with a little lemon pepper, then top with a slice of chèvre. Return to the grill, and cook until the chèvre becomes golden. Remove from the grill.
3. Cover the bowl area (the centre) of 4 small plates with rock salt. Garnish the rims with a dusting of paprika, then place each oyster in the centre of each plate. Serve immediately.

SCALLOP RAVIOLI WITH KAFFIR LIME SAUCE

Serves 4
Preparation time: 20 minutes
Cooking time: 5–7 minutes

1 egg, beaten lightly
Ravioli paste
125 g (4 oz) strong flour
1 large egg
a pinch of salt
1 tablespoon sunflower oil
1 teaspoon sesame oil
2 tablespoons semolina
Filling
175 g (6 oz) scallops
3¹/₂ tablespoons cream
a pinch of salt
Sauce
200 ml (7 fl oz) dashi 1 (page 20)
3 kaffir lime leaves
¹/₂ teaspoon dried lemon grass
2 teaspoons ginger juice
1 tablespoon Kikkoman soy sauce
1 tablespoon cornflour, diluted with water

Kaffir lime leaves are available from most Asian food shops.

1. Place all the ravioli paste ingredients in a food processor, and using the pastry blade, mix to a smooth dough. Take the ravioli dough out of the food processor and knead on a floured surface until the dough becomes very tight – very important for ravioli. Allow to rest for 30 minutes.

2. For the filling, simply put all the ingredients in a food processor, and using a cutting blade blend to a smooth paste. Take out of the food processor and put in a small bowl.

3. Roll out the ravioli paste on a floured surface as thinly as possible. Should you have a pasta roller then use it on the grade 2 thickness.

4. Using a 6 cm (2¹/₂-inch) pastry cutter, cut out 16 circles of ravioli dough. Lay 8 on the floured surface, spoon the scallop filling evenly into the centre of each ravioli, taking care to leave at least a 1¹/₂ cm (¹/₂-inch) circumference border uncovered with scallop filling. Egg wash the borders of the ravioli bases then lay the remaining 8 ravioli circles on top of the bases. Seal the edges of each ravioli with your fingers.

5. Bring a large pan of salted water to the boil. Add the ravioli, and cook for 5 minutes until the ravioli paste becomes al dente.

6. Pour all the sauce ingredients except the diluted cornflour into a pan. Bring to the boil, then reduce the heat to a simmer.

7. Cook the sauce for a further 5 minutes before thickening with the diluted cornflour. Pour the sauce through a fine sieve into a clean bowl.

8. Drain the ravioli when cooked, then place two raviolis on four warmed plates, coat with a little sauce, and serve.

SMOKED TOFU AND SOY BATTER BREAD

Serves 4–6
Suitable for vegetarians
Preparation time: 2 hours
Cooking time: 30 minutes

4¹/₂ tablespoons Kikkoman soy sauce
1 medium-size onion, chopped finely
3 teaspoons dried yeast granules
200 ml (7 fl oz) warm water
300 g (10 oz) plain flour, plus extra
for sprinkling
2 tablespoons melted butter, plus extra
1 egg
50 g (2 oz) Gruyère cheese, grated
200 g (7 oz) wholemeal flour
200 g (7 oz) block of smoked tofu
20 g (³/4 oz) sliced spring onions
1 tablespoon sesame seeds

1. Heat the soy sauce in a pan and add the onion. Cook slowly until soft but not brown.
2. In a large bowl, mix the dried yeast with the water which should be just warm. Sprinkle with a little flour. Place in a warmish area for 10–15 minutes until bubbles appear on the floured surface.
3. Now add the melted butter, egg and grated cheese. Beat well using a whisk.
4. Mix in both flours and beat well with your hand. Add the onion and soy sauce mixture. Mix once more.
5. Cover with a tea towel and place in a warmish area until the mixture doubles in size.
6. Knock back the dough, scrape it from the sides and knead on a floured surface to a smooth ball. Press out the dough with the palm of your hand, making it into a rectangle. Crumble the smoked tofu and sliced spring onions on the dough. Roll up as for a swiss roll. Place on a greased baking sheet. Cover with a tea towel, and allow to double in size in a warmish place for around 40–50 minutes.
7. Preheat the oven to Gas Mark 5/190°C/375°F.
8. Brush the roll with melted butter, and sprinkle it with the sesame seeds.
9. Bake for 30 minutes until golden.

Smoked Tofu and Soy Batter Bread

POACHED CHICKEN DUMPLINGS

Serves 4–5
Preparation time: 35 minutes
Cooking time: 10 minutes

Dough for wrappers
250 g (8 oz) plain flour
a pinch of salt
100 ml (3¹/₂ fl oz) plus 1–2
tablespoons warm water
Chicken filling
500 g (1 lb) chinese leaves
250 g (8 oz) minced chicken
2 tablespoons finely chopped spring
onions
¹/₂ teaspoon ginger juice
1 tablespoon Kikkoman soy sauce
1 tablespoon mirin or dry white wine
1 tablespoon sesame oil
4 spring onions, chopped, to garnish

Poached Chicken Dumplings

1. To make the wrappers, place the flour and salt into a bowl. Add the warm water slowly. Mix to a dough then knead on a floured surface until the dough is no longer sticky. Cover with a damp cloth, and rest it for 30 minutes.

2. Roll the dough into a long cylinder 3 cm (1 inch) in diameter. Cut into 50 even pieces. Press the dough to flatten it, then roll each piece into a thin 6 cm (2¹/₂-inch) pancake.

3. To make the filling, cook the chinese leaves in plenty of boiling salted water. Drain. Cut them into fine dice. Wrap in a tea towel or muslin cloth and wring out.

4. Mix together well the chinese leaves, chicken, spring onions, ginger juice, soy sauce, mirin and sesame oil.

5. Place a teaspoon of filling into the centre of a wrapper. Fold over and seal the edges with your fingers. Repeat for each dumpling.

6. Bring a large pan of salted water to the boil. Add the dumplings one by one. Bring to the boil once more. Add one cup of cold water and lower the heat a little.

7. When the water comes to the boil for a third time, the dumplings should float to the surface. They take approximately 5 minutes to cook. Remove from the water with a slotted spoon.

8. Place the dumplings on a large warm plate. Garnish with spring onions, and serve with soy sauce, rice vinegar and hot bean or chilli paste.

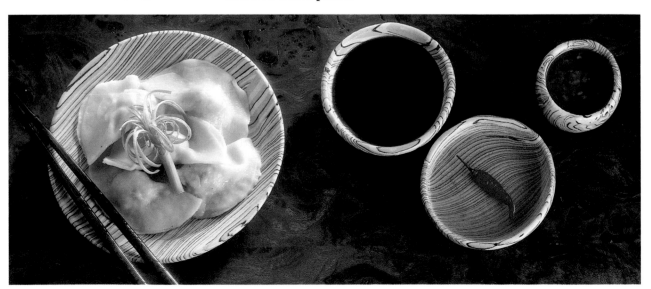

FISH DISHES

MONKFISH AND SCALLOP KEBABS

Serves 4
Preparation time: 15 minutes
Cooking time: 10 minutes

4 spring onions
500 g (1 lb) monkfish fillets, skinned
and boned
8 queen scallops
4 egg whites
a little cornflour
10 tablespoons bonito flakes
oil for deep-frying
Sauce
2 tablespoons Kikkoman soy sauce
3¹/2 tablespoons water
2 teaspoons lime juice
2 teaspoons ginger juice
2 teaspoons honey
a pinch of chilli powder
2 teaspoons cornflour diluted with
water

1. Cut away the root end of the spring onions then cut each spring onion into 4 equal lengths.
2. Slice the monkfish fillet into 8 equal-sized cubes.
3. Using bamboo kebab skewers, first skewer a piece of monkfish, followed by a piece of spring onion, then a scallop.
4. Lightly whisk the egg whites. Roll the kebabs in the cornflour, then dip into the egg whites followed by the bonito flakes. Make sure the kebabs are well coated with bonito flakes.
5. Heat the oil until a cube of day-old bread turns golden in a few seconds. Deep-fry the kebabs until golden.
6. Prepare the sauce by placing all the sauce ingredients except the cornflour in a small pan. Bring to the boil, then thicken slightly with the diluted cornflour.
7. Pour the sauce into the centre of a warmed serving plate. Top with the kebabs and serve with boiled white rice and a little chilli sauce.

GREEN-LIPPED MUSSELS WITH LEMON GRASS AND MIRIN

Serves 4
Preparation time: 10 minutes
Cooking time: 15 minutes

1 kg (2 lb) cleaned fresh green-lipped mussels
2 sprigs of lemon grass
100 ml (3½ fl oz) saké
100 ml (3½ fl oz) mineral water, sparkling or still
3 tablespoons mirin
1 garlic clove, crushed
2 teaspoons honey
2 tablespoons chopped shallot
3 tablespoons Kikkoman soy sauce
a little diluted cornflour

1. Scrub the mussels thoroughly under fresh water.
2. Crush the root of the lemon grass. Place in a large pot with all the other ingredients except for the mussels and cornflour. Cover with a lid and bring to the boil.
3. Put the cleaned mussels into the boiling broth. Again cover with the lid. Cook over a high heat for 10 minutes, until all the mussel shells have opened. Remove from the sauce and keep warm.
4. Strain the broth through a sieve into a small pan. Bring the sauce to the boil once more and thicken with a little diluted cornflour. Pour over the warm mussels to serve.

TIP If any mussels do not open, discard them. Mollusc seafoods should never be eaten if the shells do not open when cooked.

SEAFOOD AND VEGETABLE TEMPURA

Serves 4
Preparation time: 25 minutes
Cooking time: 15 minutes

1 quantity tempura batter (page 78)
4 baby squid
150 g (5 oz) tuna fillet, cut into 4
1 courgette
½ red pepper
1 small carrot
4 small pieces dried wakame, soaked
50 g (2 oz) plain flour
oil for deep-frying
8 king prawns
50 g (2 oz) udon noodles
4 strips of nori
Condiments
1 tablespoon grated ginger
3 tablespoons grated daikon
125 ml (4 fl oz) tempura dipping sauce (page 21)

Tempura is a Japanese culinary technique that was perfected after early European traders had visited Japan.
1. Prepare the tempura batter (see page 78).
2. Clean the baby squid (see page 46).
3. Slice the courgette into ½ cm (¼-inch) thick slices and the red pepper into diamonds, then cut the carrot into thin slices lengthways, so as to create ribbon-like slices.
4. Drain the wakame and pat dry with a tea towel.
5. Dust the vegetable slices and wakame with flour, dip them into the batter, then shake off any excess batter.
6. Heat the oil until a cube of day-old bread turns golden in a few seconds. Fry the vegetable slices and wakame in hot oil until golden. Remove and drain on kitchen paper.
7. Repeat the same process with the tuna, prawns, and squid.
8. Divide the noodles into 4. Dampen the nori strips with water and wrap each strip around the base of each bunch of noodles. Dip the noodles in batter and deep-fry in the usual manner.
9. Arrange the tempura seafoods and vegetables on Japanese-style serving dishes if you have them, making sure that the fried fan of fine udon noodles is displayed upright. Serve immediately with the condiments.

SQUID CHRYSANTHEMUM

Serves 4
Preparation time: 30 minutes
Cooking time: 15 minutes

8 medium-size squid tubes
1 litre (1³/4 pints) dashi 1 (page 20)
Sauce
200 ml (7 fl oz) mineral water
¹/2 teaspoon hoisin sauce
3 tablespoons Kikkoman soy sauce
¹/2 teaspoon grated fresh ginger
1 garlic clove
12 Asian lily flower stalks
12 carrot fish, cut from thin slices of
carrot using a fish cutter
a little sherry
4 x 6 cm (2¹/2-inch) pieces wakame
seaweed, soaked
arrowroot diluted with a little water
2 spring onions, sliced finely

1. Pull off the outer purple membrane from the squid then wash it. Cut open the squid into sheets, then cut in half width-ways. Cut thin strips three-quarters of the way into each width of squid (like a frill).

2. Roll one frill of squid then join the next frill onto it. Roll that, and continue with the next 2, so that 4 pieces of squid make each flower. Secure each base of the flowers with 2 toothpicks. Place the squid on a tray.

3. When the dashi comes to the boil, place the squid in it and allow to simmer for about 5 minutes. Remove the squid when cooked. Each will have the appearance of a chrysanthemum.

4. To make the sauce, boil the water, add all the ingredients except the arrowroot and spring onions, and cook for 4 minutes.

5. Thicken the sauce to an oil-like consistency with the diluted arrowroot. Finally add the sliced spring onions.

6. Pour the sauce and its garnish onto 4 warm plates. Place the squid chrysanthemums on the sauce to serve.

TIP This dish can be prepared in almost no time at all, and is a handy one to remember when you are entertaining and are short of time. Asian lily flower stalks are available from any good Asian food shop.

Squid Chrysanthemum; Green-lipped Mussels with Lemon Grass and Mirin (page 51); Seafood and Vegetable Tempura (page 51)

STEWED FISH - UMANI

Serves 4
Preparation time: 15 minutes
Cooking time: 15 minutes

50 g (2 oz) hijiki, soaked
600 ml (1 pint) fish stock or water
250 ml (8 fl oz) mirin or dry white wine
250 g (8 oz) lotus root, diced finely
100 g (3¹/2 oz) bamboo shoots, diced finely
1 kg (2 lb) monkfish fillet, skinned and boned
1 tablespoon Kikkoman soy sauce
salt

The lotus root and bamboo shoots are easily bought canned, but the hijiki is best bought dried.
1. Cook the hijiki in boiling water for 30 minutes.
2. Put the fish stock, mirin, lotus root, bamboo shoots and hijiki in a large pan, and bring to the boil. Turn down the heat to just below a simmer.
3. Cut the monkfish into walnut-size pieces, and season with the soy sauce.
4. Gently cook the monkfish in the stock with the other ingredients until the fish pieces are soft to the touch. Season with salt.
5. Serve into warm bowls.

TIP Hijiki seaweed is very fine-textured, and lends itself easily to many soups, fish and chicken dishes. It's full of protein and vitamins but has a low calorific value.

JAPANESE FISHCAKES

Serves 4
Preparation time: 15 minutes
Cooking time: 10 minutes

200 g (7 oz) cooked short-grain rice
200 g (7 oz) cooked or smoked fish
2–3 spring onions, sliced finely
1 tablespoon Kikkoman soy sauce
freshly ground black pepper
1 egg, whisked lightly
100 ml (3¹/2 fl oz) sunflower oil

These fishcakes are best made with smoked eel, but almost any fish will do.
1. Mix together the cooked rice, fish, spring onions, soy sauce, pepper and enough egg to bind the mixture thickly.
2. Heat the oil in a large frying pan, and spoon in the mixture. Flatten each slightly with the spoon.
3. Turn the fishcakes over to brown the other side.
4. When cooked, remove from the pan and dry with paper towels.

TIP A nice accompaniment for these fishcakes is plum chutney. Its sweetness blends beautifully with the delicate flavour of the fishcakes.

GRILLED MACKEREL WITH GINGER

Serves 4
Preparation time: 40 minutes
Cooking time 12 minutes

1 large mackerel
Marinade
3 tablespoons Kikkoman soy sauce
1 tablespoon grated ginger
1 garlic clove, crushed
2 tablespoons mirin
2 tablespoons saké
1 tablespoon caster sugar

Ask your fishmonger to gut the mackerel. This will save time and avoid mess.

1. Using a dessertspoon, scrape the scales off the mackerel in a tail to head motion. Once the scales are removed, cut off the head and discard it. Now wash the mackerel in plenty of cold water.

2. Put the mackerel on a clean chopping board. Using a large knife cut into 4 cm (1¹/2-inch) steaks, discarding the tail.

3. Mix all the marinade ingredients together, and marinate the mackerel steaks for 30 minutes.

4. Preheat the grill. Lay the fish steaks on a grilling tray and grill for 5 minutes, then turn them over.

5. Brush with the remaining marinade and continue to grill for 6 minutes or until the steaks are soft to the touch. Serve immediately.

GRILLED EEL

Serves 4
Preparation time: 10 minutes
Cooking time: 30 minutes

2 eels, filleted but not cut up
Seasoning
3 tablespoons Kikkoman soy sauce
3 tablespoons mirin
1 tablespoon caster sugar
1 tablespoon saké
a pinch of sansho pepper

In Japan small speciality restaurants serving only eel can be found: they provide a vast array of eel only dishes.

1. Cut the eel fillets into 8 pieces, 10–12 cm (4–5 inches) long.

2. Thread the eel pieces onto 2 bamboo skewers through their sides.

3. Place the eel kebabs on a plate or tray, and steam in a steamer for 15 minutes only.

4. Now grill the eel kebabs under a hot grill for 5 minutes, grilling them for 2¹/2 minutes on each side.

5. Mix all the seasoning ingredients together and stir well until the caster sugar dissolves.

6. Using a pastry brush, glaze the eel fillets with the seasoning mixture. Cook each side for a further 8 minutes. Reglaze the eel fillets every 2 minutes with the seasoning mixture.

7. Serve with boiled or steamed white rice and a sprinkling of sansho pepper.

SCALLOP NOVELTY

Scallop Novelty

Serves 4
Preparation time: 30 minutes
Cooking time: 5–10 minutes

400 g (13 oz) scallops
1 egg white
1/4 small garlic clove
a pinch of salt
a small pinch of Cayenne pepper
1/2 egg white
lemon juice of 1/4 lemon
8 capers

1 carrot, peeled
a small can of bamboo shoots
1/8 cucumber
2 dark shiitaki mushrooms, or a piece
of nori
50 g (2 oz) butter
100 g (3 1/2 oz) soaked birds' nest, or 2
tablespoons cooked harusame noodles,
chopped finely
125 ml (4 fl oz) dashi 1 (page 20)
1/2 egg white, whisked lightly

Dried and cleaned birds' nest can be purchased from many Asian grocers, and should be soaked in water until soft before use. Alternatively, you can use harusame (bean thread) noodles instead.

1. Place the scallop white parts, reserving the roes, and the next 4 ingredients into a food processor, blend until smooth, spoon into a bowl and place in the refrigerator.

2. Place the pink scallop roes, the half egg white, salt and lemon juice in the food processor without cleaning it, and blend until smooth. Spoon into another bowl and place in the refrigerator.

3. Wash the capers to remove the strong salty brine flavour. Slice the carrot and bamboo shoots, using a small sharp knife.

4. Shape the carrot like a fish tail, cutting out 'V' shapes to finish it. Repeat with the bamboo shoot, shaping it like a dorsal fin.

5. Cut a thick slice of cucumber then slice it in half. Cut thin slices three-quarters of the way through, to make a fan.

6. Slice the shiitake mushroom or nori seaweed into long thin strips, and leave to one side.

7. To assemble the fish, first grease 4 Chinese soup spoons or large serving spoons with soft butter.

8. Fill each spoon with the white scallop mixture, leaving space at the end for the 'head', and level the top with a knife. Then spread the remaining white mixture along the centre of each spoon, so as to form a slight dome shape.

9. Spread the pink scallop mixture over the end of the spoon to make the head of the fish.

10. Position the carrot tail, bamboo dorsal fin, cucumber ventral fin, caper eyes and nori gill as in the photograph.

11. Cover the white scallop mixture with the birds' nest or harusame noodles.

12. Keeping the spoons level, place in a steamer, and steam for 5–10 minutes until firm to the touch and cooked.

11. Prepare the sauce by heating the dashi in a small saucepan, and then stirring in the egg white. Season with a little salt.

12. Pour the sauce onto 4 warmed plates. Place the Scallop Novelties in the centres, and then serve.

PRAWNS WITH CHILLI SAUCE

Serves 4
Preparation time: 15 minutes
Cooking time: 15 minutes

12 king prawns
3 tablespoons vegetable oil
1 teaspoon fresh ginger, cut in julienne strips
1 small garlic clove, crushed
3 chillies, de-seeded and chopped finely
2 tablespoons sliced spring onions
Shrimp sauce
2 tablespoons Kikkoman soy sauce
1 tablespoon sugar
a pinch of salt
3 tablespoons tomato ketchup
1 teaspoon hot chilli sauce
1/2 teaspoon sesame oil
4 tablespoons water
1 teaspoon cornflour, diluted with water
freshly ground black pepper

1. Shell and de-vein the prawns by making a small incision along the back of the prawn with a small knife. Wash out the dark vein under cold running water.

2. Place the prawns in a bowl with the vegetable oil, ginger, garlic and chillies. Marinate and refrigerate for 3–4 hours.

3. Remove the prawns from the marinade and reserve it for future use. It will keep in the fridge for at least a month.

4. Position the prawns evenly in a roasting pan. Cook under the grill for 2–3 minutes on each side.

5. Heat in a small pan the soy sauce, sugar, salt, tomato ketchup, chilli sauce, sesame oil, water and black pepper. Bring to the boil and thicken a little with the diluted cornflour.

6. Place the prawns on a large plate and pour the sauce into a small bowl. Use the sauce as a dipping sauce.

TIP Should you prefer the sauce to be less spicy, simply add 1/2 teaspoon of chilli sauce instead of 1 teaspoon.

OYSTER FONDUE–KAKI-NABE

Serves 4
Preparation time: 20 minutes
Cooking time: 10 minutes

32 oysters
2 tablespoons salt
4 shiitaki mushrooms
1 bunch enoki mushrooms, fresh or bottled
4 spring onions
1/4 head of chinese leaves
2 bunches of edible chrysanthemum leaves
3 tablespoons red miso
1 tablespoon Kikkoman soy sauce
1 tablespoon mirin
800 ml (1 1/3 pints) dashi 1 (page 20)
12 cm (4 1/2-inch) length of konbu seaweed
4 eggs, whisked lightly (optional)

If you enjoy oysters this is a dish you simply must try. It originates, I am told, from Hiroshima, whose coastal waters are filled with oyster-beds. Oysters are to be found on many Japanese dinner tables and on the menus of many restaurants, sometimes in the form of this delicious stew.

1. Open the oysters using a sharp knife. Fill a medium-sized bowl with cold water, add the salt, then scrape the oysters out of their shells and into the cold salted water. Swill the oysters around, which will whiten and wash them. Remove and place in a small serving bowl.

2. Cut away the tough stalks from the shiitaki mushrooms. Trim the stalks from the enoki mushrooms if you are using fresh ones, and discard.

3. Cut the spring onions into 4 cm (1 1/2-inch) lengths.

4. Slice the chinese leaves into 3 cm (1 1/2-inch) widths and arrange all the vegetables and the chrysanthemum leaves in separate piles on a tray.

5. Mix together the miso and the soy sauce, mirin and 4 tablespoons dashi.

6. Spread this paste over the sides and bottom of a portable multi-purpose frying pan or electric cooker if you have one. You can place the electric cooker, if you are using one, in the centre of your dining table.

7. Position the konbu seaweed in the bottom for the next stage and add the remaining dashi.

8. Bring the dashi to the boil, whisking as it begins to simmer and then boil. When the miso has been fully whisked in, turn down the heat until it just simmers.

9. Divide the oysters between your guests, who now dip the oysters and vegetables of their choice into the hot dashi to cook. The oysters will only take a minute, whereas the vegetables will take a few minutes more.

10. Use the raw eggs as a dipping sauce if you wish.

TIP Try eating this dish using chopsticks!

BAKED HALIBUT WITH SOY SAUCE

Serves 4
Preparation time: 10 minutes
Cooking time: 25 minutes

2 lb (1 kg) halibut fillet
2 tablespoons sunflower oil
1 leek, sliced
1 smallish onion, diced finely
1 teaspoon sugar
1 carrot
1 stick of celery
2 small garlic cloves, crushed
100 ml (3 1/2 fl oz) Kikkoman soy sauce
salt and freshly ground black pepper

Sometimes it's good to be able to come home and cook a simple meal that doesn't take too long.

1. Skin the halibut fillet with a long sharp knife, cut out the vein of bones, then cut into walnut-size cubes.
2. Preheat the oven to Gas Mark 4/180°C/350°F.
3. Heat the sunflower oil in a saucepan. Add the leek and onion, cook until golden, then add the sugar. Cook for a further few minutes to caramelise the sugar.
4. Mince the carrot and celery together, or put them in a food processor, and mix well with the leek and onion.
5. Add the cubed halibut. Season with the crushed garlic, salt and pepper.
6. Pour over the soy sauce, and cook in the oven for 20 minutes, or until the fish is soft to the touch.

SALMON TERIYAKI

Serves 4
Preparation time: 15 minutes
Cooking time: 8–10 minutes

4 x 175 g (6 oz) salmon fillets, skinned and boned
1 tablespoon sunflower oil
4 sprigs of watercress
2 tablespoons grated daikon
Teriyaki sauce
1 teaspoon caster sugar
1 teaspoons saké or dry white wine
1 tablespoon mirin
2 tablespoons Kikkoman soy sauce

Grilled salmon tastes fabulous with teriyaki sauce. It is simple to prepare, and served with a little grated daikon, it makes a wonderful healthy meal for all the family.

1. Mix all the teriyaki sauce ingredients together until the sugar dissolves.
2. Marinate the salmon in the teriyaki sauce for 10–15 minutes. Drain, reserving the sauce.
3. Brush the marinated salmon fillets with the sunflower oil. Place on a grilling rack skin-side up. Grill for 4–5 minutes until slightly golden. Then using a fish slice, turn the salmon fillets over and grill for a further 4–5 minutes.
4. Serve immediately on warmed plates. Garnish with the watercress sprigs and serve with the grated daikon as a condiment in a small bowl.

JASMINE TEA-SMOKED SWORDFISH

Serves 8–10
Preparation time: 20 minutes
Cooking time: 30–35 minutes

Marinade
300 g (10 oz) rock salt
200 g (7 oz) brown sugar
2 kaffir lime leaves, bruised
1.5 kg (3¹/₂ lb) swordfish or shark
Smoking mixture
1 cup rice
1 cup brown sugar
1 cup jasmine tea
2 kaffir lime leaves

It's so easy! Try it with avocado.

1. Mix together the rock salt, brown sugar and 2 bruised kaffir lime leaves. Marinate the swordfish or shark in this overnight, then wash it off.

2. Mix together the rice, sugar and tea, and place in the bottom of a tin-foil-lined pan or wok. One layer of foil is sufficient, and there is no need to line the lid of the wok.

3. Place the swordfish on the steaming tray at least 2–3 inches above the rice, sugar and tea. Add the two kaffir lime leaves. Seal the pot or wok with a lid and damp tea towels.

4. Place on a high heat for 8 minutes and then on a low heat for 20–25 minutes.

5. Remove the swordfish from the smoke and allow to cool. Slice to serve.

TIP A good idea when smoking fish or poultry is to take the pot or wok outside when removing the lid, because the aroma caused by smoking is quite strong.

Other fish with dense flesh, such as salmon, are ideal for this cooking method. A wonderful variation is to smoke a whole chicken. Marinate it, then smoke for a full hour.

Jasmine Tea-smoked Swordfish

TUNA AND PARROT-FISH WITH BURNT SAFFRON

Serves 4
Preparation time: 5 minutes
Cooking time: 10 minutes

100 g (3 oz) clarified butter
4 fillets parrot-fish, scaled and boned
4 x 80 g (3 oz) of tuna
zest and segments of 1 lime
180 ml (6 fl oz) chicken jus (optional)
150 g (5 oz) unsalted butter
2 g saffron
1 dessertspoon tomato concassé (page 34)
salt and freshly ground black pepper
a little fresh chervil to garnish

Ask your fishmonger to scale and bone the fish.

1. Heat the clarified butter in a frying pan. Season the fish, and add to the pan skin-side down. Use two pans if necessary.
2. Blanch the lime zest in boiling salted water or in a microwave.
3. Heat the chicken jus.
4. Once the fish is golden on one side turn over to cook the other. The fish will be soft to the touch when cooked. Remove it from the frying pan and put onto the serving plates.
5. Drain the clarified butter from the pan, and add the fresh unsalted butter and the saffron. Return to the heat, cook until the butter and the saffron turns a hazelnut brown colour, then remove the frying pan from the heat, add lime juice, lime zest and tomato concassé. Spoon a little over each portion of the cooked fish.
6. Garnish with chervil.

TIP Chicken jus is stock which has been reduced and lightly thickened with cornflour and arrowroot. Adding this optional sauce makes the flavour of the whole dish richer and more refined.

Tuna and Parrot-fish with Burnt Saffron

MEAT DISHES

MARINATED CHICKEN STEAMED IN SAKÉ

Serves 4
Preparation time: 15 minutes
Cooking time: 20 minutes

4 x 200 g (7 oz) chicken breasts
Marinade and steaming liquor
3 cm (1-inch) piece of fresh ginger
250 ml (8 fl oz) saké
3 tablespoons Kikkoman soy sauce
Condiments
1/2 cucumber, sliced
a few drops of sesame oil
2 teaspoons wasabi

If economy is a consideration, use chicken legs instead of chicken breasts, and increase the cooking time by 10 minutes.
1. Finely grate the ginger, then squeeze out the ginger juice with your fingers into a bowl. Add the saké and soy sauce and mix well.
2. Add the chicken breasts to the bowl and marinate them for 20 minutes.
3. Remove the chicken and place in a steamer. Pour the reserved marinade into the bottom of the steamer. Cover with the lid and turn onto a high heat.
3. When it starts to steam, lower the heat a little. Steam the chicken breasts for 15–20 minutes and then remove them, reserving the steaming liquor.
4. Allow the chicken breasts to cool a little, then slice each breast into 7 pieces.
5. Slice the cucumber finely and mix in the sesame oil and seasoning. Serve the cucumber and wasabi condiments to accompany the chicken, and use as a dipping sauce.

TIP Remember to check the liquid level in your steamer frequently. If the liquid level is low, top it up with some hot water.

DUCK BREAST JAPANESE-STYLE

Serves 4
Preparation time: 20 minutes
Cooking time: 20 minutes

4 x 200 g (7 oz) duck breasts
2 teaspoons honey
2 tablespoons sunflower oil
Marinade
1 garlic clove, crushed
1 teaspoon grated ginger
2 tablespoons Kikkoman soy sauce
2 kaffir lime leaves
1 tablespoon honey
3 tablespoons red food colouring
Sauce
1 teaspoon hoisin sauce
2 lemon grass stalks, crushed
1 teaspoon ginger juice (page 39)
150 ml (1/4 pint) mineral water,
sparkling or still
2 teaspoons cornflour diluted with
water
Stir-fry
1/2 can of bamboo shoots
1/2 bunch of spring onions
1 tablespoon sunflower oil
250 g (8 oz) beansprouts
1 tablespoon sweet pickled ginger,
sliced finely
1 teaspoon sesame oil
salt

1. Mix all the marinade ingredients together in a stainless steel or glass bowl.

2. Place a duck breast flesh-side down on a chopping board. Using a sharp knife make cuts through the duck skin at regular 1 cm (1/2-inch) distances lengthways and then crossways so as to create a diamond-like pattern. This will allow the duck fat to render down. Repeat this process with the remaining duck breasts.

3. Brush the honey over the duck breasts, add to the marinade, cover with cling film, and refrigerate for 2 hours or overnight if you have time.

4. Drain the duck breasts, reserving the marinade for the sauce.

5. Place all the sauce ingredients except the cornflour in a small pan and bring gently to the boil. As the sauce boils thicken with the diluted cornflour. The sauce should have the pouring consistency of oil. Pour the sauce through a fine sieve into a clean bowl or jug.

6. To cook the duck breasts, heat the oil in a large frying pan, and place them in it skin-side down. Cook until the skin darkens, for 4–5 minutes, turn them over and continue cooking for a further 4–5 minutes. Remove the breasts from the pan and keep warm.

7. Cut the bamboo shoots and spring onions into 5 cm (2-inch) matchsticks. Heat the tablespoon of sunflower oil in a frying pan or wok. Add the bamboo shoots, beansprouts, spring onions and pickled ginger. Stir-fry for 2–3 minutes, and season with sesame oil and salt.

8. Pour the sauce onto 4 warmed plates.

9. Put a large spoon of stir-fried vegetables in the centre of each plate. Top the vegetables with a duck breast. Serve immediately.

STIR-FRIED BEEF WITH CHINESE LEAVES

Serves 2
Preparation time: 15 minutes
Cooking time: 15 minutes

250 g (8 oz) beef rump or fillet
Marinade for beef
1/2 teaspoon saké
1/4 teaspoon Kikkoman soy sauce
1/2 teaspoon sugar
1/2 teaspoon sesame oil
1 egg yolk

250 g (8 oz) chinese leaves
3 tablespoons vegetable oil
1 tablespoon cornflour
2 tablespoons oyster sauce
1/2 teaspoon sesame oil
1/4 teaspoon sugar
1 tablespoon cold water
salt and freshly ground pepper

1. Slice the beef into thin slices about 5 or 6 cm (2–2^1/2 inches) in length. Place in a bowl with all the marinade ingredients, and marinate for 1 hour.
2. Cut the chinese leaves into 7 cm (2-inch) lengths. Heat one tablespoon of oil in a frying pan, add the chinese leaves and stir-fry until tender. Season them, and arrange on the bottom of a large plate.
3. Drain the beef from the marinade and mix the cornflour into the beef.
4. Heat the remaining 2 tablespoons of oil in a wok or frying pan, and stir-fry the beef until golden. Remove from the wok and keep warm.
5. Add the oyster sauce to the wok, and when it begins to bubble, return the beef to the wok, and add the sesame oil, sugar and water. Stir well as the beef thickens the sauce.
6. Arrange the beef on top of the chinese leaves to serve.

Stir-fried Beef with Chinese Leaves; Pork and Shiitake Meatloaf (page 66);
Chicken Teriyaki (page 66)

CHICKEN TERIYAKI

Serves 4
Preparation time: 10 minutes
Cooking time: 20 minutes

4 x 200 g (7 oz) chicken breasts
2 tablespoons vegetable oil
4 sprigs of watercress
100 g (3¹/2 oz) grated daikon
Teriyaki sauce
4 teaspoons saké
2 tablespoons mirin
4 tablespoons Kikkoman soy sauce
2 teaspoons caster sugar

Teriyaki is a wonderful sauce; its versatile flavour allows it to marry with fish, shellfish and almost any white meat.
1. Mix all the sauce ingredients in a bowl, until the sugar dissolves. Place the chicken breast in the marinade for 5 minutes then remove and drain.
2. Heat the vegetable oil in a frying pan, place the breast skin-side down and cook for 7 minutes, then turn over to cook the other side. Cook until the breasts are firm to the touch.
3. Once the breasts are cooked, drain off the excess oil and pour in the Teriyaki sauce. Cook for a further few minutes until the chicken is well coated with the sauce.
4. Serve with watercress and the grated daikon for a condiment.

TIP You can use Kikkoman Teriyaki sauce instead.

PORK AND SHIITAKI MEATLOAF

Serves 4
Preparation time: 20 minutes
Cooking time: 40–50 minutes

oil for greasing
500 g (1 lb) minced pork (shoulder or leg)
250 g (8 oz) cream cheese
50 g (2 oz) crumbled blue cheese
200 g (7 oz) shiitaki mushrooms, diced finely
1 tablespoon Kikkoman soy sauce
1 teaspoon Worcestershire sauce
1 tablespoon mild French mustard
1 egg
1 teaspoon dried sage

Meatloaves these days tends to be regarded as a little old-fashioned. This is a pity because not only are they hearty and good tasting, they are also easy and economical to prepare.
1. Preheat the oven to Gas Mark 4/180°C/350°F.
2. Quite simply place all the ingredients in a large bowl. Mix well with a wooden spoon. Then place in a greased terrine or mould into a loaf shape and wrap in well-greased tin foil. Bake in the oven for 40–50 minutes until cooked. Allow to rest for 5 minutes before unwrapping and slicing.

TIP Serve the meatloaf hot or cold with rice or salad and pickles, or turn it upside-down, brush with honey and colour it under a hot grill.

THAI MEATBALLS FLAVOURED WITH KAFFIR LIME LEAVES AND CHILLIES

Serves 4
Preparation time: 20 minutes
Cooking time: 15 minutes

Meatballs
500 g (1 lb) chicken mince
1 egg white
2 tablespoons finely diced onion
1/2 chilli, diced finely
2 teaspoons grated ginger
2 teaspoons crushed garlic
oil for brushing
4 kaffir lime leaves, bruised
salt and finely ground black pepper
Sauce
100 ml (31/2 fl oz) water
250 g (8 oz) peanut butter
1 tablespoon honey
2 tablespoons Kikkoman soy sauce
8 drops hot chilli sauce
1/2 teaspoon sesame oil
1/2 bunch of spring onions, sliced finely

1. Preheat the oven to Gas Mark 5/190°C/375°F.
2. Mix all the meatball ingredients together with the exception of the kaffir lime leaves. Season with salt and pepper.
3. Using your hands roll into small walnut-sized balls.
4. Place the balls in a roasting tray brushed with a little oil. Add the kaffir lime leaves to the roasting tray. Cover with foil. Bake in the oven for 15 minutes until firm to the touch.
5. To make the sauce, heat the water in a small pan, add the peanut butter, honey, soy sauce, hot chilli sauce and sesame oil, and stir constantly as the sauce heats up.
6. Once hot, place the meat balls in a serving bowl, pour over the peanut sauce and finally sprinkle with the spring onions.

TIP This dish is inexpensive to make, and the meat balls freeze well. Try serving it another way by using the sauce as a dip. Simply dip the meat balls into the sauce, much like a fondue.

TONKATSU

Serves 4
Preparation time: 10 minutes
Cooking time: 10 minutes

4 x 100 g (31/2 oz) pork loin slices
flour for dusting
2 eggs, lightly beaten
75 g (3 oz) breadcrumbs
corn oil for frying
1/2 lemon, cut into 4 wedges
salt and freshly ground black pepper
Dipping sauce
3 tablespoons saké
3 tablespoons tomato sauce
2 teaspoons Worcestershire sauce
2 tablespoons Kikkoman soy sauce
2 teaspoons mild mustard
1 teaspoon chilli sauce or hot chilli sauce

Tonkatsu is a loin cut of pork, coated with breadcrumbs and deep-fried. It is enormously popular in Japan and is eaten by millions every day.
1. Place the slices of pork in a large clear plastic bag, then place on a chopping board. Gently bat out the pork slices with a meat mallet, so that they are around 1/2 cm (1/4-inch) thick.
2. Season the pork slices, then dust them all over with flour.
3. Dip the slices into the beaten eggs, then dip them into the breadcrumbs. Pat the pork slices so that the crumbs stick firmly.
4. Heat the oil in a pan, then fry the pork slices 2 at a time for 5 minutes. Remove when golden on both sides, then drain on paper towels.
5. Whisk all the sauce ingredients together in a small bowl.
6. Slice the Tonkatsu into 2 cm (3/4-inch) pieces. Serve with the lemon wedges and the dipping sauce.

CHICKEN AND SPRING ONION KEBABS WITH PEANUT BUTTER SAUCE

Serves 4
Preparation time: 20 minutes
Cooking time: 15 minutes

4 chicken breasts
2 teaspoons sesame oil
1 tablespoon Kikkoman soy sauce
8 spring onions
3 tablespoons sunflower oil
Peanut butter sauce
1 tablespoon butter
2 shallots, diced finely
1 garlic clove, crushed .
150 ml (1 1/4 pint) warm water
3 tablespoons Kikkoman soy sauce
5 tablespoons smooth peanut butter
hot chilli sauce to taste

1. Cut the chicken breasts into walnut-size pieces and season with the sesame oil and soy sauce.
2. Cut the spring onions into 4 cm (1¹/2-inch) lengths. Then place the chicken pieces and spring onion pieces alternately onto kebab sticks. Make 8 in total.
3. Heat the oil in a frying pan and cook the kebabs for 10 minutes or until cooked.
4. To make the sauce, melt the tablespoon of butter in a saucepan, and add the shallots and garlic. Cook until soft, but not brown. Pour in the water, soy sauce, and peanut butter and whisk until smooth. Bring to the boil and season with hot chilli sauce.
5. Serve the kebabs, with or without white rice, topped with the peanut butter sauce.

FIVE SPICE SPARE RIBS

Serves 4
Preparation time: 10 minutes
Cooking time: 40–50 minutes

1 kg (2 lb) pork spare ribs
4 tablespoons liquid honey
3 tablespoons sunflower oil
spring onions, chopped, to garnish
Marinade
2 teaspoons five spice powder
4 garlic cloves, crushed
1/4 teaspoon Cayenne pepper
1 tablespoon grated ginger
125 ml (4 fl oz) Kikkoman soy sauce
3 tablespoons sunflower oil

1. Ask your butcher to cut through each spare rib.
2. Place the spare ribs in a large pan or bowl. Mix the marinade ingredients together and pour over the ribs, stirring well. Cover with the marinade overnight. Drain when ready to cook, reserving the marinade.
3. Heat the oil in a large frying pan and fry the spare ribs in small amounts, so that they seal well. Place the sealed ribs in a large pot with the marinade. Cook covered with a lid over a medium heat until the meat on the ribs becomes tender.
4. Remove the lid, add the honey and reduce the sauce a little so that it becomes a little thicker and glazes the ribs.
5. Serve as they are or with boiled rice.

Chicken and Spring Onion Kebabs with Peanut Butter Sauce; Duck Breast Japanese-style (page 63); Five Spice Spare Ribs

ROAST CHICKEN WITH VEGETABLE-FILLED JACKET POTATOES

Serves 4
Preparation time: 15 minutes
Cooking time: 1 hour

1 kg (2 lb) chicken
2 tablespoons sunflower oil
1 teaspoon paprika
1/2 teaspoon marjoram
2 tablespoons Kikkoman soy sauce
2 large onions
4 baking potatoes
25 g (1 oz) butter
2 medium-size onions, sliced thinly
2 thin slices cooked ham, chopped
125 g (4 oz) button mushrooms, sliced thinly
salt and freshly ground black pepper

1. Preheat the oven to Gas Mark 4–5/180–190°C/350–375°F.
2. If using a frozen chicken, wash it inside and out in cold water, then dry with some paper towels.
3. Mix the oil, paprika, marjoram and soy sauce together in a bowl, then brush all over the chicken, both inside and out.
4. Roughly slice the two large onions, and place them flat on the bottom of the roasting pan. Place the chicken on top. This will prevent the chicken from sticking to the roasting pan.
5. Cook for 1 hour or until cooked. Baste the chicken every 20 minutes.
6. Prick the cleaned potatoes a few times with a fork. Wrap in foil and bake at the same time as the chicken.
7. Melt the butter in a pan. Add the medium-size onions, cover with a lid and cook until soft, but not brown.
8. Add the ham and mushrooms to the cooked onions. Cook for a further 5 minutes.
9. Test the potatoes to see if they are cooked, using a skewer. Remove the foil, then cut each in half. Mash the inside a little with a fork. Then top each with a little of the onion, mushroom and ham mixture. Serve with the roast chicken.

STEAMED PORK IN BAMBOO

Serves 4
Preparation time: 10 minutes
Cooking time: 20 minutes

150 g (5 oz) minced pork leg
200 ml (7 fl oz) water or chicken stock
25 g (1 oz) canned bamboo shoots, chopped finely
1 teaspoon spring onion, chopped finely
1 1/2 teaspoons Kikkoman soy sauce
1/4 teaspoon salt

The hollow bamboo cooking moulds impart an exotic flavour into the mince pork. They are made from a large bamboo cane, that has been cut into 8 cm (5-inch) lengths, just above the ring marks. Bamboo cane is available at many Asian food stores. Pyrex bowls or small soufflé dishes will also serve the purpose.
1. If you are using a water-bath, preheat the oven to Gas Mark 4/180°C/350°F.
2. Place all the ingredients in a food processor, and blend to a smooth purée.
3. Pour the pork purée into 4 bamboo cooking moulds, or other similar-size moulds.
4. Place in a steamer for 20 minutes or cook in a water-bath in the oven until the purée is firm to the touch. Serve while still hot.

TANDOORI CHICKEN

Serves 4
Preparation time: 30 minutes
Cooking time: 20 minutes

8 chicken drumsticks
1/4 teaspoon salt
2 tablespoons lemon juice
2 tablespoons red food colour
lemon wedges and chopped onion to serve
Marinade
100 ml (3 1/2 fl oz) natural yogurt
1 1/2 tablespoons Kikkoman soy sauce
2 teaspoons white vinegar
1/2 tablespoon fresh ginger, grated finely
2 garlic cloves, crushed
1/2 teaspoon cardamom powder
1/4 teaspoon cinnamon
1/2 teaspoon ground white pepper
1/2 teaspoon chilli powder
1 teaspoon nutmeg
1 teaspoon cumin powder
1 teaspoon coriander
sunflower oil

1. Using a sharp knife cut slits down each drumstick. Mix the salt, lemon juice and red food colour together. Coat the chicken drumsticks, then rest them for 20 minutes.
2. Mix together the yogurt and spices. Strain through a sieve over the drumsticks. Cover with cling film and refrigerate overnight.
3. Preheat the oven to Gas Mark 4/180°C/350°F. Line an ovenproof dish with foil, place the drumsticks in it side by side and pour over the marinade.
4. Cover with a lid or foil, and bake for 40 minutes.
5. Serve hot with white rice, the lemon wedges and chopped onions.

MARINATED BEEF

Serves 4
Preparation time: 15 minutes
Cooking time: 12–15 minutes

250 g (8 oz) beef rump, sliced thinly
6 spring onions
Seasoning for beef
1 tablespoon Kikkoman soy sauce
1 1/2 tablespoons saké or dry white wine
1 1/2 tablespoons sunflower oil
a pinch of freshly ground black pepper
Sauce
1 tablespoon Kikkoman soy sauce
2 teaspoons rice vinegar
1 garlic clove, crushed
2 teaspoons sesame oil
2 tablespoons sunflower oil
1 teaspoon chilli paste

Ask your butcher to slice the beef thinly.
1. Mix all the beef seasoning ingredients together and add the beef. Marinate for 10 minutes.
2. Mix together all the sauce ingredients in a separate small bowl.
3. Slice the spring onions diagonally into 1 cm (1/2-inch) pieces.
4. Heat a wok or large frying pan, add the beef and stir-fry for 5 minutes, or until cooked. Then add the spring onions, and stir-fry for 1 more minute. Add the sauce, and mix well before transferring the beef to a serving bowl.

FAR EASTERN PORK CASSEROLE

Serves 4–5
Preparation time: 15 minutes
Cooking time: 1 hour 10 minutes

6 tablespoons Kikkoman soy sauce
1 kg (2 lb) rindless pork loin or leg
1 teaspoon paprika
5 tablespoons sunflower oil
275 ml (9 fl oz) mineral water,
sparkling or still
1 red pepper, sliced finely
2 carrots, sliced finely
1 small savoy cabbage, sliced finely
1 medium-size onion, sliced finely
125 g (4 oz) button mushrooms
200 g (7 oz) beansprouts
1 small can of pineapple pieces
a pinch of Cayenne pepper
1 tablespoon cornflour diluted with
water

Far Eastern Pork Casserole

1. Cut the pork into walnut-size pieces, or ask your butcher to do this for you.
2. Mix 1 tablespoon of the soy sauce with the paprika and the pork.
3. Heat 3 tablespoons of the sunflower oil in a large saucepan. Add the pork and sear on each side in the hot oil until golden. This will help prevent flavour escaping.
4. Now add the water and the remaining 5 tablespoons of soy sauce. Cover and cook slowly in a moderate oven for 25 minutes.
5. After 30 minutes add the pepper, carrots, cabbage and onion and add more water if necessary. Cook for a further 25 minutes.
6. After 50 minutes of cooking the pork should begin to soften. Now add the button mushrooms, beansprouts and pineapple pieces, season with the Cayenne pepper, and bring to the boil. Simmer for 5 minutes then thicken with a little diluted cornflour.
7. Serve from the saucepan into bowls.

TIP If you would like the sauce a little sweeter, add the juice from the pineapple pieces to it. This recipe can if necessary feed up to 8 people.

SUKIYAKI

Serves 4
Preparation time: 15 minutes
Cooking time: 10 minutes

400 g (13 oz) beef, sirloin, rump or
tenderloin
200 g (7 oz) shirataki noodles
200 g (7 oz) tofu
8 shiitaki mushrooms
2 leeks
100 g (3¹/₂ oz) spinach
4 eggs
3–4 x 2 cm (1-inch) beef suet cubes
Warishita stock
2 tablespoons sugar
3 tablespoons saké or dry white wine
3 tablespoons mirin
100 ml (3¹/₂ fl oz) Kikkoman soy
sauce
100 ml (3¹/₂ fl oz) water

Sukiyaki

Sukiyaki is a wonderful dish, suitable for the whole family. It is inexpensive and quick to prepare.

1. Cut the beef into thin 1 cm (¹/₂-inch) lengths.
2. Blanch the shirataki noodles in boiling water for 2 minutes, then drain in a colander.
3. Cut the stems off the shiitaki mushrooms, and discard. Cut the leeks diagonally into 2 cm (1-inch) lengths. Cut the spinach in half.
4. Arrange the beef and prepared vegetables decoratively on a large plate.
5. Crack the eggs into separate bowls, and whisk each a little.
6. Mix all the warishita stock ingredients together.
7. Heat a wok or frying pan, add the suet, cook until half melted, add the sliced beef and stir-fry.
8. When half cooked, add three-quarters of the warishita stock, tofu, prepared vegetables and the shirataki noodles, and continue to cook until the vegetables are tender. Serve into 4 bowls.
9. Sukiyaki is eaten by dipping the cooked foods in the bowl of egg before being eaten.

TIP Should you have only a small wok or frying pan then cook the Sukiyaki in smaller batches.

MANDARIN PANCAKES WITH TWO FILLINGS

Serves 6
Preparation time: 25 minutes
Cooking time: 15–20 minutes

Pancake dough
300 g (10 oz) plain flour
a pinch of salt
150 ml (¹/4 pint) hot water
1 teaspoon sesame oil
2 tablespoons sunflower oil

Pork and beansprouts filling
1 teaspoon mirin or dry white wine
1 teaspoon Kikkoman soy sauce
¹/2 teaspoon cornflour
100 g (3¹/2 oz) lean pork loin or fillet, sliced thinly
4 tablespoons sunflower oil
100 g (3¹/2 oz) spring onions, chopped
1 tablespoon mirin or dry white wine
250 g (8 oz) beansprouts
1 tablespoon Kikkoman soy sauce

Spinach and bean thread noodles filling
2 tablespoons sunflower oil
500 g (1 lb) spinach
50 g (2 oz) bean thread noodles
5 tablespoons water
2 tablespoons Kikkoman soy sauce

This amount of dough is sufficient for both the Pork and Beansprouts and the Spinach and Bean Thread Noodles fillings.

1. Place the flour and salt in a bowl and add the hot water slowly. Mix to a dough, then knead until the dough is no longer sticky. Cover with a damp cloth and allow to rest for 20–30 minutes.

2. Roll out the dough on a floured surface then roll up into a long cylinder 3 cm (1¹/2 inches) in diameter. Cut into 24 pieces. Roll each into an 8 cm (3-inch) circle.

3. Brush the surface of each circle with the sesame oil. Place two oiled sides together, making 12 rounds. Roll out each round to a pancake 18 cm (7 inches) in size. The pancakes must be very thin.

4. Heat the sunflower oil in a frying pan and fry each pancake, turning over once when the surface begins to bubble. Remove from the hot oil.

5. Be sure to separate the pancakes from each other whilst still hot. Cover with a cloth and keep warm until served.

6. If you have chosen the pork filling, mix the mirin or dry white wine, the soy sauce and the cornflour together, and stir in the thin slices of pork. Marinate for 5 minutes.

7. Heat 2 tablespoons of the sunflower oil in a wok. Stir-fry the beansprouts quickly. Remove them and keep warm.

8. Heat the remaining 2 tablespoons of sunflower oil, and stir-fry the pork until golden.

9. Add all the rest of the ingredients except the beansprouts, reheat, and add the beansprouts. Tip into a warm serving bowl.

10. If you have chosen the spinach filling, pull off the spinach stems, and cut the leaves into 5 cm (2-inch) lengths.

11. Soak the bean thread noodles in warm water until soft. Drain, then cut into 5 cm (2-inch) lengths.

12. Heat the sunflower oil in a wok, and stir-fry the spinach quickly.

13. Add the bean thread noodles, water and soy sauce. Reheat, then tip into a warm serving bowl.

14. To serve, simply place the fillings in the middle of the table with the pancakes and let your family or guests help themselves.

TIP These pancakes can be frozen if you place a sheet of clingfilm or greaseproof paper between each one.

NECK FILLET OF LAMB WITH SPRING ONIONS, SESAME SEEDS AND HONEY

Serves 4
Preparation time: 20 minutes
Cooking time: 15 minutes

1 tablespoon sunflower oil
4 neck fillets of lamb
8 spring onions, cut in half
1 tablespoon Kikkoman soy sauce
100 g (3¹/2 oz) unsalted butter
juice of ¹/2 lemon
1 tablespoon finely diced red pepper
1 tablespoon finely diced yellow pepper
1 tablespoon finely diced green pepper
1 tablespoon roasted peanuts
1 teaspoon fresh ginger, grated
1 tablespoon fresh coriander, chopped
1 tablespoon runny honey
1 teaspoon toasted sesame seeds

1. Heat the sunflower oil in a large frying pan. Sauté the lamb until golden all over.
2. Add the spring onions and soy sauce. Cook for a further 5 minutes until the fillets are just firm to the touch.
3. Cook the unsalted butter in a separate pan to a nut brown colour. Add the lemon juice, diced peppers, peanuts, grated ginger, chopped coriander and honey. Remove from the heat.
4. Place the neck fillets and spring onions on a warm serving plate. Coat with the sauce. Sprinkle with toasted sesame seeds and serve.

TIP Neck fillets of lamb are tender, inexpensive and very versatile.

SOY BEANS COOKED WITH CHICKEN WINGS

Serves 4
Preparation time: 40 minutes
Cooking time 35–40 minutes

300 g (10 oz) dried soy beans
500 g (1 lb) chicken wings
1 small leek
1.5 litres (2¹/2 pints) cold water, plus extra
1 tablespoon sunflower oil
1¹/2 cm (¹/2-inch) piece of fresh ginger, sliced finely
Marinade for chicken wings
1 tablespoon Kikkoman soy sauce
1 tablespoon saké or dry white wine
Seasoning
1 tablespoon caster sugar
2 tablespoons saké or dry white wine
4 tablespoons Kikkoman soy sauce

1. Wash the soy beans in cold water, and soak overnight in the water.
2. Mix the marinade ingredients together and pour over the chicken wings. Marinate for 30 minutes, stirring occasionally.
3. Slice the leek into 1 cm (¹/2-inch) pieces.
4. Place the soy beans and water in a saucepan, bring to the boil, and add another 100 ml (3¹/2 fl oz) of water. Repeat twice more. This process will help the soy beans to cook and soften a little quicker. Continue cooking for an hour or until the soy beans become soft.
5. As the soy beans cook, skim off the surface residue with a ladle.
6. Using a wok or large frying pan, heat the oil and fry the sliced ginger. Add the chicken wings, and cook until golden. Now add the leek and cook for 2 minutes.
7. Pour the cooked soy beans onto the chicken wings and add enough water to cover both. Return to the heat, and simmer for 15 minutes.
8. Mix together the seasoning ingredients, add them and cook for 2 more minutes. Serve in warm bowls.

TEPPANYAKI

Serves 4
Preparation time: 25 minutes
Cooking time: 20 minutes

1 leek
¹/2 green pepper
¹/2 yellow pepper
1 pork fillet
2 x 200 g (7 oz) chicken breasts,
skinned and boned
400 g (13 oz) beef fillet
60 g (2¹/2 oz) beansprouts
1 tablespoon sunflower oil
Condiments
grated ginger
grated daikon
1 lime cut into wedges
Kikkoman soy sauce

Teppanyaki uses the Japanese style of grilling: meat, fish and vegetables are all grilled in the same way. Some Japanese restaurants serve wonderful Teppanyaki: the chef actually grills the food in front of you.

1. Cut the leek diagonally into ¹/2 cm (¹/4-inch) slices. Cut the yellow and green peppers into diamonds.

2. Put all the condiments in separate bowls onto a Japanese-style tray or a large serving plate.

3. Slice the pork fillet, chicken breast and beef fillet into ³/4 cm (¹/4-inch) slices, and arrange the meats decoratively on the tray or plate.

4. The ideal cooking method for Teppanyaki at home is to use an electric frying pan placed in the centre of a dining table so that your guests can select and cook their own choice of the meat and vegetables. Alternatively, you can use a large thick-bottomed frying pan as the taste will be just as good.

5. Cooking the Teppanyaki is very simple. Brush the bottom of the frying pan with oil, and put in the vegetables, being careful not to cover the bottom of the frying pan. Leave a little space between each piece. Cook for 3–5 minutes, then remove from the frying pan and keep warm.

6. Add the sliced meats to the frying pan, again not too close together. When golden on both sides serve immediately with the grilled vegetables and condiments.

Teppanyaki

VEGETABLE, RICE AND TOFU DISHES

TEMPURA BATTER

Suitable for vegetarians
Preparation time: 5 minutes

500 g (1 lb) vegetables, sliced or
500 g (1 lb) meat or fish, cubed
plain flour for dusting
oil for deep-frying
Batter 1
3 egg yolks
400 ml (14 fl oz) iced water
250 g (8 oz) plain flour
Batter 2
1 whole egg
150 ml (¹/4 pint) iced water
125 g (4 oz) plain flour

A tempura consists of deep-fried slices of vegetables, or cleaned pieces of meat or fish, which have first been dipped in flour, then coated in a light batter and deep-fried. My experiences with Japanese cooking have revealed many tempura batter recipes. The following two were given to me by Japanese chefs, and both produce wonderful tempura that is both light and crisp. Experiment with both to find out which you prefer.

If you are making batter 1:-
1. Lightly whisk the egg yolks and add the iced water, gently whisking as you do so.
2. Add the flour, whisking the mixture once again. Do not whisk the mixture until it is smooth; if anything, leave the batter a little lumpy.

If you are making batter 2:-
1. Lightly whisk the whole egg and the iced water.
2. Add the flour all at once and whisk it quickly. Again, do not whisk the mixture until it is completely smooth; if anything, leave the batter a little lumpy.

FRIED CELERIAC STRAW

Serves 4
Suitable for vegetarians
Preparation time: 15 minutes
Cooking time: 5 minutes

1 large bulb of celeriac
oil for deep-frying
salt

Use this celeriac in salads, instead of croûtons, or as a nibble with pre-dinner drinks, or try it under some fried fish or chicken. Its texture is similar to potato but it is somewhat sweeter to eat.

1. Using a large knife, cut away the outer skin of the celeriac, then slice a little off each side, to form a cube. This allows the celeriac to sit firmly as you slice it finely into thin sheets.
2. Spread these sheets along your chopping board, like a deck of cards. Slice again into thin matchstick-like pieces.
3. Wash the celeriac in cold running water, then allow to soak in cold water for 1 hour. Drain and dry the celeriac in a tea towel.
4. Heat the oil until a cube of day-old bread turns golden in a few seconds. Deep-fry the celeriac until golden. Drain away any excess frying fat and season with salt.

FRIED LEAF SPINACH

Serves 4
Suitable for vegetarians
Preparation time: 5 minutes
Cooking time: 6 minutes

2 tablespoons soya oil
350 g (11¹/2 oz) spinach
1 garlic clove, crushed
1 tablespoon spring onions, sliced finely
salt
¹/2 teaspoon caster sugar (optional)

Spinach is a wonderfully nutritious food that is full of vitamins and is easily digested.

1. Wash the spinach in cold water. Cut into 7–8 cm (2³/4–3 inch) lengths (do not remove the stalks as Europeans tend to do).
2. Heat the oil in a wok or large frying pan. Add the spinach, garlic and spring onions. Stir over a high heat until tender. Season with salt and a little sugar. Serve in a warm china bowl.

EGG AND TOFU CURRY

Serves 4
Suitable for vegetarians
Preparation time: 15 minutes
Cooking time: 25 minutes

2 tablespoons sunflower oil
1/2 onion, diced finely
4 teaspoons mild curry powder
1/2 teaspoon cumin
1/4 teaspoon caraway seeds
4 teaspoons flour
1/2 clove garlic, crushed
1/2 tablespoon tomato purée
400 ml (14 fl oz) hot water
1 tablespoon Kikkoman soy sauce
200 g (7 oz) firm tofu
4 eggs
1 tablespoon chopped fresh coriander

1. Heat the sunflower oil and add the finely diced onion. Cook until soft but not brown. Then turn up the heat, add the curry powder, cumin and caraway seeds, and fry for 20 seconds, then turn down the heat.
2. Add the flour, garlic and tomato purée and stir to a semismooth paste. Continue cooking for a further 3 minutes, then remove from the heat to cool a little.
3. Once the flour and curry roux has cooled a little, stir in the hot water and soy sauce a little bit at a time until a sauce consistency is reached. Return to a moderate heat and cook for 10 minutes.
4. Preheat the oven to Gas Mark 3/160°C/325°F.
5. Cut the tofu into large pieces and add to the curry sauce. Then pour the whole mixture into one large ovenproof dish, or 4 smaller individual ovenproof dishes.
6. Crack an egg into each dish and sprinkle with coriander. Cover with a lid or tin foil. Bake for 10 minutes.
7. Serve from the ovenproof dishes with boiled white rice.

TIP If using a large single oven dish cook for a further 5–10 minutes.

EGG FRIED RICE

Serves 4–6
Suitable for vegetarians
Preparation time: 15 minutes
Cooking time: 10 minutes

3 tablespoons sunflower oil
2 eggs, beaten lightly
1 kg (2 lb) cooked rice, cooled
1/4 red pepper, diced finely
1/4 green pepper, diced finely
250 g (8 oz) beansprouts
salt
1/2 bunch spring onions, sliced finely

Rice is closely associated with most forms of Asian cookery. It has been part of the staple diet in Asia for thousands of years.
1. Heat the oil in a wok or large frying pan. Add the eggs, and cook for 1 minute.
2. Add the rice and peppers, stir-fry until the rice softens and becomes hot. Add the beansprouts and stir-fry for a further 2 minutes.
3. Season with salt to taste, and serve in a large bowl, garnished with sliced spring onions.

Egg and Tofu Curry; Deep-fried Cauliflower with Lime (page 82); Egg Fried Rice

DEEP-FRIED CAULIFLOWER WITH LIME

Serves 4
Suitable for vegetarians
Preparation time: 15 minutes
Cooking time: 10 minutes

1/2 head cauliflower, boiled or steamed
l lemon or lime
2 sheets of rice paper
oil for deep-frying
a little flour
salt and freshly ground pepper
lemon or lime quarters to serve
Batter
150 g (5 oz) flour
250 ml (8 fl oz) chilled water
1 egg yolk

The batter used for the cauliflower can be used for almost any vegetable. You could try broccoli, mushrooms, spring onions or other vegetables.

1. To make the batter, place all the ingredients in a bowl and whisk to a smooth paste. Keep chilled in the refrigerator.
2. Heat the oil until a cube of day-old bread turns golden in a few seconds.
3. Cut the cauliflower into small heads. Dip into the seasoned flour. Shake off any excess flour, then coat with the batter. Deep-fry until golden. Serve on the rice paper with either lemon or lime quarters.

EGG NOODLES FRIED WITH VEGETABLES

Serves 4
Suitable for vegetarians
Preparation time: 15 minutes
Cooking time: 10 minutes

150 g (5 oz) dried egg noodles
1/2 teaspoon sesame oil
1 small carrot
65 g (2 1/2 oz) canned bamboo shoots
1/2 stick of celery
4 shiitaki mushrooms
3 tablespoons sunflower oil
2 tablespoons spring onions, sliced finely
Seasoning
1 tablespoon Kikkoman soy sauce
1 teaspoon saké or dry white wine
1 teaspoon ginger juice
1 teaspoon sesame oil

1. Cook the egg noodles in plenty of boiling salted water until tender, about 10–15 minutes. Rinse under plenty of cold running water, and add the sesame oil.
2. Cut the carrot, bamboo, celery and shiitaki mushrooms into fine matchstick-like pieces.
3. Heat the oil in a wok or large frying pan. Stir-fry the sliced vegetables for 1 minute, then add the cooked egg noodles. Heat through before adding all the seasoning ingredients.
4. Transfer to a large serving bowl. Garnish with sliced spring onions, and serve.

SWEET POTATOES

Serves 4
Suitable for vegetarians
Preparation time: 15 minutes
Cooking time: 1 hour

4–5 sweet potatoes
100 g (3¹/2 oz) unsalted butter, plus
extra for greasing
250 g (8 oz) light brown sugar
a pinch of cinnamon
2 tablespoons Kikkoman soy sauce
150 ml (¹/4 pint) pineapple juice
¹/4 teaspoon salt

Sweet potatoes are known as kumera in New Zealand and Australia and yams in America. Whatever they are called, you must try them – they are delicious.

1. Preheat the oven to Gas Mark 5/190°C/375°F.
2. Peel the sweet potatoes with a small knife. Slice into 1 cm (¹/2-inch) pieces.
3. Brush an earthenware bowl with butter. Lay the slices of sweet potato inside. Put on a few knobs of butter, and sprinkle the sugar and cinnamon between each layer of potatoes.
4. Mix together the soy sauce, pineapple juice and salt. Pour over the potatoes, and cover with a lid. Bake for 1 hour until cooked.

HASH BROWNS

Serves 4
Suitable for vegetarians
Preparation time: 45 minutes
Cooking time: 5 minutes each

750 g (1¹/2 lb) potatoes, such as maris
piper or cara
a pinch of dried thyme
a pinch of salt
ground black pepper
50 g (2 oz) butter
4 teaspoons Kikkoman soy sauce

There are so many delightful ways to enjoy hash browns. My favourites are: two hash browns, one topped with a fried egg and the other with a piece of fanned avocado; or just one hash brown topped with avocado, smoked salmon and hollandaise sauce. Both need a grind of black pepper from a pepper mill.

1. Boil or steam the unpeeled potatoes in their skins until soft. Once cooked cool down overnight.
2. Peel off the skin with a small knife, then coarsely grate the potatoes. Season with the dried thyme, salt and pepper.
3. Heat a little butter in a small pan. Divide the potato into 8 small balls or 4 larger ones.
4. Place the potato balls into the hot pan and press down to flatten. Cook each side until golden.
5. Season with 1 teaspoon each of soy sauce and serve.

STIR-FRIED VEGETABLES

Serves 4
Suitable for vegetarians
Preparation time: 15 minutes
Cooking time: 10 minutes

1/4 head of chinese leaves
100 g (3 1/2 oz) mushrooms or shiitake mushrooms
250 g (8 oz) carrots
1/4 head of cauliflower, cut into florets
250 g (8 oz) baby corn, halved if large

3 tablespoons soya oil
250 g (8 oz) onions, sliced finely
100 g (3 1/2 oz) beansprouts
1 teaspoon sesame oil
2 tablespoons Kikkoman soy sauce
1 teaspoon grated fresh ginger
1/2 garlic clove, crushed
1/2 red pepper, chopped
100 g (3 1/2 oz) mangetout
salt

1. Cut the chinese leaves into 2.5 cm (1-inch) square pieces. Slice the mushrooms 3 mm (1/2-inch) thick.
2. Peel the carrots, and cut into matchstick-like slices.
3. Cut the cauliflower florets into quarters.
4. Heat the soya oil in a wok or large frying pan over a high heat. Add the onions, carrots and cauliflower, and stir-fry for 2–4 minutes.
4. Add the remaining ingredients and continue to stir-fry over a high heat, until the vegetables are cooked. The overall cooking time should be no longer than 10 minutes. This should ensure the vegetables are crisp.

TIP This dish can be finished with the addition of 100 ml (3 1/2 fl oz) of chicken stock or water and 2 tablespoons of Kikkoman soy sauce. Add these liquids to the vegetables and heat through. Thicken with a little cornflour diluted with water. This finishing touch makes the stir-fry more moist, which is sometimes more appealing.

Stir-fried Vegetables

VEGETABLE MOUSSES

Serves 4
Suitable for vegetarians

Carrot
200 g (7 oz) cooked carrot purée
2 whole eggs
5 dessertspoons double cream
a pinch of caster sugar
a pinch of salt and freshly ground black
pepper

Beetroot
200 g (7 oz) cooked beetroot purée
2 whole eggs
4 dessertspoons double cream
2 tablespoons malt vinegar
a pinch of caster sugar
a pinch of salt and freshly ground black
pepper

Red pepper
200 g (7 oz) red pepper peeled and
cooked
5 dessertspoons double cream
2 whole eggs
a pinch of Cayenne pepper
a pinch of salt and freshly ground black
pepper

Spinach
200 g (7 oz) cooked spinach
4 egg whites
4 dessertspoons double cream
a pinch of nutmeg
a pinch of caster sugar
a pinch of salt and freshly ground black
pepper

Pumpkin
200 g (7 oz) cooked pumpkin purée
4–5 dessertspoons double cream
2 whole eggs
a pinch of nutmeg
a pinch of caster sugar
a pinch of salt and freshly ground black
pepper

Choose any of the vegetable flavours, or make several mousses for a larger party.

1. To make the vegetable purée(s), dice and steam or boil until soft, for 5–10 minutes, with the exception of the spinach, which should be boiled for 3 minutes, drained, and immediately cooled in iced water.

2. Preheat the oven to Gas Mark 3/160°C/325°F.

3. Place all the ingredients of the mousse you have chosen in a food processor or blender, and blend until smooth. Season to taste.

4. Pour into buttered timbales or small soufflé dishes. Poach in a water-bath in the oven until firm to the touch, about 15–20 minutes.

5. Test by inserting a skewer into the centre of each mousse. If it comes out clean, the mousse is cooked. Turn out of the moulds to serve. These mousses can be eaten hot or cold.

Vegetable Mousses

BRAISED PUMPKIN

Serves 4
Suitable for vegetarians
Preparation time: 5 minutes
Cooking time: 25–30 minutes

500 g (1 lb) kabocha or pumpkin
1 very small chilli
2 tablespoons caster sugar
2 tablespoons Kikkoman soy sauce
100 ml (3 1/2 fl oz) mineral water,
sparkling or still

Although Japanese pumpkins – kabocha – are difficult to obtain, they are more suitable for this dish than British ones because of their softer flesh. However an ordinary one is perfectly acceptable.

1. Cut the unpeeled pumpkin into 8 pieces, discarding the seeds.
2. Bring a pan of salted water to the boil. Add the chilli and the pumpkin pieces and cook for 15 minutes or until a wooden skewer will only just pass through the pumpkin.
3. Drain the pumpkin in a colander. Return to the pan with the remaining ingredients, cover with a lid and simmer for a further 10 minutes, or until the pumpkin is fully cooked.
4. Serve in small bowls with a little of the soy sauce cooking liquor.

AUBERGINES WITH MISO

Serves 4
Suitable for vegetarians
Preparation time: 10 minutes
Cooking time: 10 minutes

500 g (1 lb) aubergines
3 tablespoons sunflower oil
1 teaspoon fresh ginger, chopped finely
2 tablespoons saké
1 teaspoon black sesame seeds
Miso seasoning
3 tablespoons white miso
2 tablespoons warm water
1 1/2 tablespoons caster sugar
2 teaspoons Kikkoman soy sauce

1. Dice the aubergines into 2 cm (3/4-inch) square pieces.
2. Heat the oil and add the aubergine and ginger. Stir-fry for 5 minutes, then reduce the heat and pour the saké over the aubergine.
3. In a small bowl mix together all the miso seasoning ingredients with a fork.
4. Pour over the aubergine, quickly mix through, then transfer to a large serving bowl. Sprinkle with black sesame seeds and serve hot.

RED BEAN RICE

Serves 8
Suitable for vegetarians
Preparation time: 4 hours
Cooking time: 1 hour

75 g (3 oz) dried red beans
700 ml (1 pint 3 1/2 fl oz) cold water
575 g (1 lb 3 oz) glutinous rice
2 tablespoons black sesame seeds

Red Bean Rice, although eaten throughout Asia, has a special significance in Japan as it is often cooked for celebrations such as weddings and festivals.

1. Wash the red beans in cold water to remove any impurities. Put in a pan with the water, and bring to a gentle simmer. Cook uncovered for 15 minutes.

2. Drain the red beans in a colander. Reserve the cooking water for later use.

3. Wash the rice 5 or 6 times, until the water becomes clear. Place it in a bowl, add half the reserved red bean water, and soak overnight if you have the time, otherwise for a minimum of 4 hours.

4. Drain the rice, and mix it with the semi-cooked red beans. Spread it out evenly on a shallow tray or plate, and place in a steamer for 15 minutes.

5. Remove the lid, and sprinkle a third of the remaining red bean cooking water over the rice. Cover once more and cook for a further 10 minutes. Repeat twice more, so that the whole cooking period totals 40–50 minutes.

6. Remove the rice from the steamer, and rest it for 5 minutes before spooning it into a serving bowl.

7. Toast the sesame seeds under a hot grill for a few seconds, then sprinkle them over the rice. Serve.

TIP Red Bean Rice can be served hot, but is most often served at room temperature.

MANGETOUT WITH CHILLI SAUCE

Serves 4
Suitable for vegetarians
Preparation time: 5 minutes
Cooking time: 5 minutes

450 g (15 oz) mangetout
1 tablespoon sunflower oil
1 garlic clove, crushed
1 tablespoon hot chilli sauce
2 teaspoons Kikkoman soy sauce

1. Pick or cut off the stalks from the mangetout.

2. Heat the oil in a wok or frying pan. Add the garlic.

3. Pour the mangetout into the wok. Stir-fry for 4–5 minutes or until the mangetout become crisp.

4. Quickly stir the chilli and the soy sauces into the mangetout. Spoon into a warmed serving bowl and serve.

STIR-FRIED SPINACH AND BEANSPROUTS

Serves 4
Suitable for vegetarians
Preparation time: 5 minutes
Cooking time: 6 minutes

300 g (10 oz) spinach
2 tablespoons vegetable oil
1/2 garlic clove, crushed
100 g (3 1/2 oz) beansprouts
1 tablespoon spring onion, sliced finely
2 teaspoons Kikkoman soy sauce
salt and freshly ground black pepper

1. Cut the spinach into 7 cm (2-inch) lengths. Heat the vegetable oil in a wok or frying pan, add the garlic, then the spinach and beansprouts.
2. Stir over a high heat until the leaves become tender, then add the spring onions, soy sauce and pepper. Serve straight from the wok.

FRIED RICE WITH CRABMEAT AND SPINACH

Serves 4
Preparation time: 10 minutes
Cooking time: 10 minutes

100 g (3 1/2 oz) spinach leaves
100 g (3 1/2 oz) cooked crabmeat, frozen or canned

1 1/2 tablespoons sunflower oil
2 eggs, beaten lightly
750 g (1 1/2 lb) cooked long grain rice
2 teaspoons Kikkoman soy sauce
3 tablespoons mineral water, sparkling or still
2 tablespoons spring onions, sliced finely

The colours in this dish are a delight.
1. Slice the spinach leaves into 1 cm (1/2-inch) strips.
2. Flake the crabmeat, removing any pieces of cartilage and shell.
3. Heat the oil in a wok or frying pan, and quickly cook the eggs and spinach.
4. Add the rice, then heat through a little more before adding the crabmeat, soy sauce, mineral water and spring onions. Stir everything thoroughly so that all flavours and ingredients are mixed well together.
5. Transfer the mixture into a large bowl, and serve.

Stir-fried Spinach and Beansprouts

STEAMED WHITE RICE

Serves 4
Suitable for vegetarians
Preparation time: 35 minutes
Cooking time: 30 minutes

European rice
2 cups long grain rice
3³/4 cups water
Japanese rice
3 cups rice
3¹/2 cups water

Rice cookers are now available in most good kitchen appliance shops throughout the West. These cookers provide excellent rice every time. If you eat or would like to eat rice more often, then a rice cooker is a good investment.

1. Wash the rice well several times until the water runs clear. Put the rice in a sieve, and leave it to drain for 30 minutes.

2. Choosing the right pan to cook your rice is most important: it should be a solid, thick-bottomed pan with a lid, large enough so that the rice only half-fills it.

3. Place the rice and water in the pan, and put on the lid. Bring to the boil over a medium heat. Once you hear the rice boiling turn up the heat so that the rice boils vigorously. Soon the lid will begin to vibrate and a whitish residue will appear. Reduce the heat to low, and continue to cook until you hear a faint sound of popping rice. Remove the pan from the heat, and rest it for 20 minutes so that the rice steams itself and becomes soft and fluffy.

4. Do not remove the lid at any point once cooking has begun, as valuable steam will be lost. Use your ears and not your eyes when cooking rice like this.

TIP In Japan rice would now be transferred to a rice tub, and would be served by the hostess using a rice paddle into individual rice bowls.

SPICED FRIED BEANS WITH GINGER

Serves 4
Suitable for vegetarians
Preparation time: 5 minutes
Cooking time: 10 minutes

450 g (15 oz) fine green beans
2 tablespoons corn oil
1 teaspoon grated fresh ginger
¹/2 teaspoon chilli paste or Tabasco
sauce
a pinch of salt

1. Using a small sharp knife, top and tail the fine green beans.

2. Heat the corn oil in a wok or frying pan, add the green beans and cook, stirring constantly.

3. Half-way through cooking, add the ginger, chilli paste or Tabasco and salt. Continue to stir-fry until the beans become crisp when tasted.

4. Remove from the wok, drain any excess oil and serve.

DIPPED TOFU

Serves 4
Suitable for vegetarians
Preparation time: 15 minutes
Cooking time: 5 minutes

300 g (10 oz) block of firm tofu
2 tablespoons potato flour
Dipping sauce
100 ml (3¹/2 fl oz) dashi 2 (page 20)
2 teaspoons mirin
2 teaspoons ginger juice (page 39)
2 tablespoons Kikkoman soy sauce
1 teaspoon hot chilli sauce

Tofu lends itself to almost any form of cooking. Its versatility is much underestimated in Europe, as is its nutritional value: it contains large amounts of protein without the calories and cholesterol found in meat.

1. Mix together all the dipping sauce ingredients in a small bowl.
2. Slice the block of tofu into 2 cm (³/4-inch) pieces, and dust with potato flour.
3. Heat the oil until a cube of day-old bread turns golden in a few seconds.
4. Deep-fry the tofu in hot oil until golden.
5. Remove the tofu squares and drain on paper towels.
6. Serve the tofu squares in small bowls. Use chopsticks to dip the fried tofu pieces into the dipping sauce before eating.

POACHED TOFU BITES

Serves 4
Suitable for vegetarians
Preparation time: 15 minutes
Cooking time: 20 minutes

a little salt
40 g (1¹/2 oz) broad beans
300 g (10 oz) block of firm tofu
4 tablespoons potato flour
2 teaspoons black sesame seeds
1 teaspoon poppy seeds
Poaching stock
300 ml (¹/2 pint) dashi 1 (page 20)
3 tablespoons Kikkoman soy sauce
2 tablespoons mirin
1 tablespoon caster sugar
1 teaspoon sesame oil

1. Bring a pan of salted water to the boil. Cook the broad beans until tender, about 10 minutes. Drain the broad beans in a colander, and cool under cold running water. Peel the skins off the beans, then dice the beans finely with a sharp knife.
2. Place the tofu in a bowl and mash it to a paste with a fork. Mix in the potato flour, diced broad beans, sesame seeds and poppy seeds.
3. Roll the tofu paste into balls the size of walnuts.
4. Mix together the ingredients for the poaching stock. Put in a wide pan and bring to the boil.
5. Poach the tofu balls in the stock for 10 minutes, then remove from the heat. Pour into 4 soup bowls and serve.

DEEP-FRIED TOFU WITH BONITO FLAKES AND SPRING ONIONS

Serves 4
Preparation time: 10 minutes
Cooking time: 5 minutes

300 g (10 oz) block of firm tofu
1 tablespoon potato flour
1 large egg, beaten lightly
1/2 packet of bonito flakes
oil for deep-frying
1 lemon cut into wedges
3 tablespoons Kikkoman soy sauce

1. Cut the tofu into 2 cm (3/4-inch) square pieces.
2. Dust the tofu squares with potato flour, and dip into the egg, then into the bonito flakes. Coat the tofu well with the bonito flakes.
3. Deep-fry the tofu squares until golden. Remove from the deep-fryer and drain on kitchen paper.
4. Serve in 4 small bowls, garnished with lemon wedges. Serve the soy sauce in small bowls as a dipping sauce.

SWEET AND SOUR BABY COURGETTES

Serves 4
Suitable for vegetarians
Preparation time: 10 minutes
Marinating time: 4 hours

16 baby courgettes
1 tablespoon salt
Sweet and sour dressing
1 garlic clove, crushed
1 tablespoon caster sugar
2 tablespoons rice vinegar
1 teaspoon chilli paste or hot chilli sauce
1 tablespoon sesame oil
2 teaspoons Kikkoman soy sauce

1. Top and tail the courgettes, and slice into 1 cm (1/2-inch) pieces. Put in a bowl, and sprinkle with the salt. Leave for 1 hour before washing off the salt in plenty of cold water.
2. Mix all the dressing ingredients together and pour over the courgettes. Cover with cling film, and refrigerate overnight or for a minimum of 4 hours. Serve.

SALADS

CRAB-STUFFED LOTUS ROOT SALAD

Serves 4
Preparation time: 20 minutes
Cooking time: 30 minutes

3 tablespoons rice vinegar
15 cm (6-inch) length of lotus root,
fresh or canned
125 g (4 oz) cooked white crabmeat
1/8 garlic clove, crushed
a pinch of Cayenne pepper
a pinch of salt
1 teaspoon mirin
1/2 egg white
1/2 cucumber, peeled and sliced
3 tablespoons Kikkoman soy sauce
1/2 teaspoon caster sugar
fresh coriander (optional)

The hollow tubes inside lotus root make it ideal for all kinds of stuffing mixtures. Don't be limited to the crab I have chosen; try it with cooked chicken, mushrooms or savoury rice.

1. Cut the lotus root in half. Peel and carve between the tubes so as to create a flower-like shape.

2. Bring a pot of water to the boil with 2 tablespoons of the rice vinegar. Cook the lotus root for 8–10 minutes. Remove the lotus root and allow to cool a little.

3. Place the crabmeat, garlic, Cayenne and salt into a food processor. Blend to a paste. Add the mirin and the half egg white. Blend once more.

4. Push the crab mixture into the tubes of the lotus root. Steam for 15 minutes until cooked. Allow to cool, then refrigerate until cold.

5. Slice the lotus root into 1 cm (1/2-inch) slices. Cover the bottom of a large plate with the cucumber slices arranged one on top of the other in a circular fashion around the edge of the plate. Neatly arrange the lotus root slices in the centre of the plate.

6. Mix the soy sauce, sugar and the remaining rice vinegar together, and dress the lotus root salad with it. Garnish with a sprig of coriander, if you wish, and serve.

Soba Salad (page 94); Smoked Chicken and Sweet Potato Salad (page 94); Crab-stuffed Lotus Root Salad

SMOKED CHICKEN AND SWEET POTATO SALAD

Serves 4
Preparation time: 15 minutes

1 leg or breast of smoked chicken
450 g (15 oz) sweet potato, boiled and then peeled
1/4 head curly endive lettuce
2 leaves radicchio lettuce
2 teaspoons sesame seeds
chopped fresh chervil
Dressing
1 tablespoon lemon juice
2 teaspoons Dijon whole grain mustard
4 tablespoons sunflower oil
1 tablespoon runny honey
salt and freshly ground black pepper

1. To make the dressing, pour the lemon juice and mustard into a bowl. Slowly whisk in the sunflower oil and honey. Season to taste. Shake or stir the dressing before use.
2. Flake or cut the smoked chicken into small pieces.
3. Slice three-quarters of the sweet potato into thin slices; finely dice the remainder. Arrange the sliced and diced sweet potato in circles in the centre of each plate.
4. Wash the lettuce and place a little of each upon the circles of sweet potato and smoked chicken. Pour a little dressing over each. Toast the sesame seeds under the grill, and sprinkle them and the chervil over the salad.

SOBA SALAD

Serves 6
Suitable for vegetarians
Preparation time: 15 minutes
Cooking time: 10 minutes

40 g (1 1/2 oz) hijiki
1 teaspoon sunflower oil
3 tablespoons Kikkoman soy sauce
15 g (1/2 oz) wakame
1 small bunch of raw spinach
1/2 bunch of watercress
200 g (7 oz) soba noodles
50 g (2 oz) beansprouts
Dressing
100 ml (3 1/2 fl oz) sunflower oil
100 ml (3 1/2 fl oz) Kikkoman soy sauce
3 tablespoons lemon or lime juice

1. Soak the hijiki in cold water for 15 minutes until tender. Rinse the hijiki in cold water to remove any impurities.
2. Heat half the oil in a saucepan. Cook the hijiki in the oil for 3 minutes, then add the soy sauce. Cook until it is reduced in size. Cool.
3. Wash the wakame in cold running water. Soak for 5 minutes in cold water. Drain it and chop it roughly.
4. Wash the spinach, drain it and slice it into fine strips. Pick the leaves from the watercress, and add them to the sliced spinach.
5. Cook the soba in plenty of boiling salted water until tender. Refresh the drained soba in cold water.
6. Place the soba noodles on a large plate. Top with the spinach, watercress, beansprouts and wakame. Shake all the dressing ingredients together in a sealable jar and sprinkle over the salad.

SOBA SALAD WITH GINGER

Serves 4
Preparation time: 15 minutes
Cooking time: 4–5 minutes

1 packet of soba noodles
100 g (3¹/2 oz) sprouted beans, such as
mung, aduki, wheat or red kidney beans
30 g (1¹/4 oz) spring onions, sliced finely
1 tablespoon toasted black sesame seeds
1 tablespoon pickled ginger, sliced finely
Dressing
200 ml (7 fl oz) dashi 1 (page 20)
1¹/2 tablespoons Kikkoman soy sauce
1 tablespoon mirin
1 teaspoon sesame oil
1¹/2 tablespoons rice vinegar or white
wine vinegar

These buckwheat noodles are available in many health food stores and Asian grocery shops. Sprouted beans are inexpensive and easy to grow at home, providing you have some sprouting trays or jars. Alternatively, health food stores, Asian grocery shops and good supermarkets also stock them.

1. Prepare the dressing by mixing all the ingredients together in a small bowl or jar and whisking with a fork, or shaking the jar.

2. Bring a large pan of salted water to the boil. Drop the soba into the boiling water and stir to make sure they do not stick together. Cook for 4–5 minutes until tender. Drain immediately, then plunge the noodles into very cold water to stop the cooking process and to cool them down. Drain once more.

3. Place the soba in a bowl, large enough to mix them with the dressing. Then sprinkle with the sprouted beans, spring onions, black sesame seeds and pickled ginger. Serve immediately.

SPRING SALAD

Serves 4
Preparation time: 15 minutes

¹/2 cucumber, peeled
1 tablespoon salt
15 g (¹/2 oz) dried wakame seaweed
80 g (3¹/4 oz) beansprouts
Dressing
1 tablespoon Kikkoman soy sauce
3 tablespoons rice vinegar
1 tablespoon mineral water, sparkling
or still
1¹/2 tablespoons caster sugar

1. Slice the cucumber finely, put in a bowl and sprinkle with the tablespoon of salt. Leave to rest for 10 minutes before washing off the salt in plenty of cold water.

2. Soak the wakame in cold water until soft, for about 5 minutes.

3. Bring a small pot of unsalted water to the boil. Dip the wakame into the boiling water for 10 seconds, then plunge into ice cold water. This will prevent the wakame from over-cooking and losing nutritional value.

4. Prepare the dressing by simply stirring all the dressing ingredients together in a small bowl until the caster sugar dissolves.

5. Place the cooled wakame on a chopping board, cut away the tough edge and discard. Cut the remaining wakame into 3 cm (1-inch) pieces.

6. Mix the cucumber, wakame and beansprouts together in a salad bowl. Pour over the dressing and serve.

GREEN BEAN SALAD WITH PEANUT DRESSING

Green Bean Salad with Peanut Dressing

Serves 4
Preparation time: 10 minutes
Cooking time: 5 minutes

300 g (10 oz) fine green beans

Peanut dressing
3 tablespoons peanut butter
1 tablespoon caster sugar
2 teaspoons Kikkoman soy sauce
5 tablespoons dashi 1 (page 20)

1. Top and tail the beans with a small knife. Cook uncovered in plenty of boiling water until crisp, about 5–10 minutes. When cooked, plunge the drained beans into ice cold water. Drain and dry once cold.
2. Prepare the dressing by placing all the ingredients into a bowl. Mix well with a whisk.
3. Toss the cooked beans with the dressing. Place in a salad bowl to serve.

TIP Cooking the beans this way is called blanching. It not only retains the beans' colour, but also much of their goodness and flavour.

GRAPEFRUIT AND AVOCADO SALAD

Serves 4
Preparation time: 15 minutes

2 ruby grapefruit
1 ripe avocado, peeled and diced
4 spring onions, sliced finely
1/4 red pepper, sliced finely

Dressing
2 teaspoons Kikkoman soy sauce
2 teaspoons lime or lemon juice
1 teaspoon caster sugar
a grind of black pepper
2 tablespoons walnut oil

1. Cut the grapefruits in half and discard any seeds. Cut around the flesh of each half and then from the middle of the outer edge, to cut segments in each half grapefruit. Place all the segments in a bowl.
2. Add the avocado pieces, the spring onions and red pepper to the bowl. Shake all the dressing ingredients together in a sealable jar and mix together with the salad. Spoon it back into each grapefruit half to serve.

PAN-FRIED AUBERGINE SALAD WITH SWEET AND SOUR SAUCE

Serves 4
Preparation time: 10 minutes
Cooking time: 10 minutes

450 g (1 lb) aubergine
3 tablespoons olive oil
30 g (1¹/4 oz) onions, diced finely
30 g (1¹/4 oz) carrots, diced finely
30 g (1¹/4 oz) celery, diced finely
100 ml (3¹/2 fl oz) Sweet and Sour
Sauce (page 31)
salt and freshly ground black pepper

This salad was recently made by a friend of mine, Bruce, using a leftover sweet and sour sauce that I had prepared. I was really impressed with the taste, so here's the recipe.

1. Cut the aubergine into large dice. Heat the olive oil in a frying pan until it smokes, add the aubergine and quickly sear it on all sides by shaking the pan so that all sides of the aubergine get a little fried. Cook for 4–5 minutes then tip out of the frying pan into a bowl. Allow to cool.

2. Add the onion, carrot and celery to the pan, gently cook over a medium heat for 5 minutes, then add to the cooling aubergine.

3. Once the vegetables are cooked, pour the cold Sweet and Sour Sauce over the salad mixture. Serve in bowls with a little crisp lettuce.

Pan-fried Aubergine Salad with Sweet and Sour Sauce

TIP Try this dish – it tastes so good, and it's something good to cook when you don't have much time.

PICKLED VEGETABLES

Serves 4
Preparation time: 15 minutes

1 medium-size carrot
1 courgette
1 small leek
1/2 red pepper
1/2 green pepper
75 g (3 oz) hijiki seaweed, soaked
Marinade
3 1/2 tablespoons rice vinegar
4 cm (1/2 inch) piece of fresh ginger,
sliced
3 tablespoons mineral water, sparkling
or still
1 tablespoon honey or caster sugar
1 teaspoon sesame oil

These finely sliced vegetables are wonderful when simply sprinkled over a salad, or quickly steamed and served with fish or chicken. They will also keep for up to a week in the refrigerator.

1. Using a sharp knife, cut off 4 edges from the carrot so as to create a long squared-shaped carrot. Now finely slice the carrot into many thin sheets. Spread out these thin sheets of carrot like a deck of cards, and slice the carrots lengthways into thin strips no more than 3–4 mm (1/8-inch) wide.

2. Repeat this same process with the courgette.

3. Cut the leek into 8 cm (3-inch) lengths. Finely slice lengthways.

4. Cut away the top and bottom of the red and green pepper halves and flatten them to create two sheets. Again, finely slice lengthways into thin strips. Reserve the tops and bottoms for a salad.

5. Mix all the marinade ingredients together in a stainless steel or glass bowl. Add all the sliced vegetables, and marinate in the refrigerator for at least 2 hours before serving.

SWEET POTATO SALAD WITH CURRY MAYONNAISE

Serves 4
Preparation time: 10 minutes
Cooking time: 40 minutes

2 medium-size sweet potatoes
1 teaspoon fresh chopped coriander
150 ml (1/4 pint) mayonnaise
1 teaspoon mild curry powder
juice of 1/2 lemon
2 tablespoons roasted peanuts

This salad will easily keep in the fridge for 3–4 days.

1. Boil or steam the sweet potatoes in their skins until cooked, usually about 35–40 minutes. Allow to cool.

2. Using a small knife, peel the skins off the sweet potatoes, then dice into 1 cm (1/2-inch) cubes, and place in a bowl.

3. Chop the coriander leaves, and add them to the sweet potatoes. Mix in the remaining ingredients. Serve on its own or with crisp lettuce leaves.

SWEETS

PICASSO ICE CREAM

The wonderful thing about this dish is that you can present it any way you like and it never needs to look the same.

1. To make the sablé biscuits, place all the ingredients apart from the egg wash and grated chocolate or nuts in a food processor and using the pastry blade, blend the mixture to a smooth pastry. Remove and place in the refrigerator to chill and solidify a little.

2. Preheat the oven to Gas Mark 6/200°C/400°F.

3. Roll out the sablé pastry 3 mm (1/4-inch) thick on a floured surface. Cut strips of pastry 10 cm (4 inches) long by 1 cm (1/2-inch) wide and put them on a baking sheet. Brush them with the egg wash and sprinkle with sugar, nuts or chocolate.

4. Bake in the oven until golden, about 10 minutes.

5. Make the fruit purées by blending the cleaned fruits separately with 1 tablespoon of caster sugar in each. Sieve the purées into small clean bowls and refrigerate until ready to use.

6. The plates should be chilled a little by putting them in the refrigerator for 20 minutes.

7. Present the dessert by first pouring streaks of the 3 different purées and chocolate sauce over each plate. Top with the balls of ice cream, meringue shells, sablé biscuits, strawberries and raspberries. Dust with icing sugar to serve.

Preparation time: 40 minutes

Sablé biscuits
250 g (8 oz) plain flour
200 g (7 oz) butter
150 g (5 oz) caster sugar, plus extra for sprinkling
1 drop of vanilla essence
1 egg yolk
1 tablespoon cream
1 egg, lightly whisked, for glazing
grated chocolate or chopped nuts for sprinkling
Fruit purées
100 g (3¹/2 oz) strawberries
100 g (3¹/2 oz) kiwi-fruit
100 g (3¹/2 oz) mango
3 tablespoons caster sugar
To serve
3 tablespoons chocolate sauce
4 balls chocolate ice cream
4 balls vanilla ice cream
4 balls strawberry ice cream
8 meringue shells
¹/2 punnet strawberries and raspberries
icing sugar

TIP The ingredients for this dessert can vary to suit your tastes. The meringue shells are easily bought in any supermarket. The important thing to remember is that this dessert should be fun, and a little outrageous.

FRESH FRUITS DEEP-FRIED WITH RAIN NOODLES

Serves 4
Preparation time: 20 minutes
Cooking time: 15 minutes

100 g (3¹/₂ oz) shirataki noodles
1 small bunch of grapes
1 peach
1 apricot
8 strawberries
1 banana
2 tablespoons cornflour
12 mint leaves
3 egg whites, whisked lightly
oil for deep-frying
whipped cream
or
tofu ice cream (page 106), optional

Shirataki noodles when deep-fried are known in America as Rain Noodles – a wonderful name!

1. Using a pair of kitchen scissors cut the shirataki noodles into 3 cm (1¹/₄-inch) lengths, and put in a bowl.

2. Divide the bunch of grapes into 4 smaller bunches.

3. Cut the peach and apricot into quarters, discard the stones, then slice each quarter in half again.

4. Remove the stalks from the strawberries.

5. Slice the banana into 12.

6. Dust all the fruits with cornflour, making sure all the sides are coated. Dip the fruits and mint into the egg whites and finally into the noodles. Coat each piece of fruit and mint with noodles.

7. Heat the oil until a cube of day-old bread turns golden in a few seconds.

8. Deep-fry the peaches and apricots first, until a wooden skewer will pass easily through each piece. Remove and keep warm.

9. Now fry the grapes and banana and remove when cooked. Finally fry the strawberries and mint.

10. Place a mixture of the 5 fruits and mint leaves onto 4 warmed plates, and serve with either whipped cream or tofu ice cream.

Apple and Rice Cake (page 102); Nashi Sorbet (page 102); Fresh Fruits Deep-fried with Rain Noodles

NASHI SORBET

Serves 4
Preparation time: 2–3 hours

4 nashi (Asian pears) or comice pears
3 tablespoons mineral water, sparkling
or still
2 teaspoons lime juice
125 g (4 oz) caster sugar
a few mint leaves

1. Peel, core and slice 3 of the nashi or pears thinly, then place in a small pan with the mineral water and caster sugar. Cover with a lid and cook over a medium heat until the nashi or pears are soft.
2. Remove the pan from the heat and push the mixture through a fine sieve into a clean bowl. Place over ice until cold, then stir in the lime juice.
3. Pour the nashi or pear mixture into an ice cream machine and freeze, or place the bowl in your freezer.
4. As the edges of the sorbet begin to freeze, quickly whisk the mixture until smooth. Continue freezing, whisking the sorbet a further 5 or 6 times until it can be scooped into balls using an ice cream scoop or spoon.
5. Cut the whole nashi or pear into 8 wedges and finely slice each into a fan. Lay the fans on a tray covered with cling film. Put in the freezer for 15–20 minutes until frozen.
6. Scoop the nashi or pear sorbet with a warm tablespoon onto 4 chilled plates. Garnish with the frozen nashi or pear fans and mint leaves and serve.

APPLE AND RICE CAKE

Serves 4–6
Preparation time: 30 minutes
Cooking time: 30–40 minutes

100 g (3¹/2 oz) short-grain rice
50 g (2 oz) sugar
500 ml (18 fl oz) milk
a few drops of rose-water
a few drops of vanilla essence
300 g (10 oz) sweet shortcrust pastry,
frozen or home-made
butter for greasing
3–4 cooking apples
1 egg, lightly whisked

1. Slowly cook the rice with the sugar in a small pan with the milk.
2. When the rice is soft and fairly dry mix in the rose-water and vanilla essence.
3. Preheat the oven to Gas Mark 3/160°C/325°F.
4. Roll out the pastry and cut into 2 circles about 15–18 cm (6–7 inches) in diameter.
5. Grease the bottom of a 15–18 cm (6–7 inch) cake tin, and line it with one circle of the pastry.
6. Slice the peeled and cored apples thinly. Layer the cake tin alternately with the rice and apple. Then seal the top with the other circle of pastry.
7. Brush with egg, and bake for 30–40 minutes until a skewer will easily pass through the cake and the pastry lid is golden.
8. Eat warm or cold with fresh cream or ice cream.

FRIED SWEET SESAME BITES

Serves 4
Preparation time: 20 minutes
Cooking time: 10 minutes

1 large egg (size 2)
100 g (3¹/₂ oz) caster sugar
1 tablespoon sunflower oil
3 tablespoons water
300 g (3¹/₂ oz) plain flour
1 teaspoon baking powder
5 tablespoons white sesame seeds
oil for deep-frying
icing sugar for dusting
whipped cream or vanilla ice cream
(optional)

1. Mix together in a large bowl the egg, caster sugar, sunflower oil, and water. Sift the flour and baking powder together and add to the bowl to make a dough. Knead till smooth on a floured surface.
2. Roll out the dough into a long sausage. Cut the dough into 20, then roll each piece between the palms of your hands into a ball.
3. Roll each ball in the sesame seeds, making sure the balls are well coated with the sesame seeds. Heat the oil to 170°C/340°F, or until a cube of day-old bread turns golden in a few seconds.
4. Deep-fry the balls until golden. Remove from the oil and dry on paper towels.
5 Place on rice paper if you wish, and dust with icing sugar to serve.
6. Europeans may like to serve these deep-fried balls with whipped cream or vanilla ice cream.

TIP Should you have difficulty making the sesame seeds stick to the dough balls, simply moisten them with a little cold water, then roll them again in the sesame seeds.

ALMOND AND SESAME BISCUITS

Makes 16
Preparation time: 15 minutes
Cooking time: 15 minutes

1 large egg (size 2), beaten lightly
100 ml (3¹/₂ fl oz) water
2 tablespoons sesame oil
3 drops of almond essence
175 g (6 oz) raisins
25 g (1 oz) sesame seeds
125 g (4 oz) caster sugar
125 g (4 oz) self-raising flour, plus
extra for sprinkling
125 g (4 oz) wholemeal flour
16 blanched almonds

1. Preheat the oven to Gas Mark 2/150°C/300°F.
2. Place all ingredients except the almonds in a food processor bowl. Using the dough hook mix to a firm dough. Remove from the bowl, and put onto a floured surface.
3. Divide the dough into 16 equal-sized balls. Place the balls on a non-stick or greased baking sheet and firmly press a blanched almond into the top of each biscuit.
4. Bake for about 15 minutes until golden. Allow to cool before eating.

LOTUS ANALISE

Serves 4–6
Preparation time: 50 minutes
Cooling time: 10 minutes

Tulip biscuit paste
75 g (3 oz) plain flour
4 tablespoons butter, plus extra for greasing
125 g (4 oz) plus 1 tablespoon icing sugar
2 egg whites
vanilla essence

Raspberry sauce
150 g (5 oz) raspberries
1 tablespoon caster sugar
2 tablespoons mineral water, sparkling or still

Rosewater mousse
175 g (6 oz) white chocolate
4 tablespoons milk
a little rose-water
5 g (1/4 oz) gelatine soaked in a little water
2 egg yolks
350 ml (12 fl oz) double cream, semi-whipped

Garnish
400 g (13 oz) caster sugar
2 tablespoons red piping jelly (optional)
100 ml (3 1/2 fl oz) water
65 g (2 1/2 oz) raspberries
4 mint leaves
65 g (2 1/2 oz) icing sugar

I wanted the book to have a finale of some kind, something that is achievable with a little practice. What better end to a lovely evening than a dessert (named after my second daughter) that looks like a flower, has the aroma of a rose and the delicate taste of freshly picked raspberries.

1. Preheat the oven to Gas Mark 5/190°C/375°F.

2. To prepare the tulip pastry leaves begin by placing all the tulip biscuit paste ingredients in a food processor. Mix until a smooth thick batter is reached. Leave to rest for 15 minutes.

3. Using a square, flat piece of plastic or cardboard draw a 6 cm (2 1/2-inch) lotus leaf in the centre then, using a sharp knife, cut out the inside of the leaf, thus creating a stencil.

4. Brush a baking sheet with butter. Lay the stencil on the baking sheet and, using a palate knife, spread with tulip biscuit paste. Remove the stencil – a lotus leaf-shape of tulip paste will remain. Repeat the same process for 40 leaves. This may require 2 or 3 baking sheets. Bake until golden. Remove the biscuits from the baking sheets using a palate knife. Lay the biscuits over the side of a tin so that they become rounded.

5. Place the raspberries, caster sugar and mineral water in a food blender and blend to a purée. Pour the sauce through a fine sieve into a small bowl, removing the seeds. Refrigerate until needed.

6. Melt the soaked gelatine in a microwave or a small pan.

7. Melt the white chocolate in a microwave or in a double boiler. Warm the milk then stir into the melted white chocolate with the rose-water and gelatine.

8. Add the egg yolks to 30 g (1 1/4 oz) of the caster sugar, and whisk together until the mixture becomes light and the sugar dissolves.

9. Fold the egg mixture into the white chocolate, then fold in the cream. Place in refrigerater for 2 hours until set.

10. Pour the remaining caster sugar into a saucepan. The sugar should come no more than half-way up the side of the pan. Mix the water into the sugar, making sure all the sugar becomes wet. Place on high heat, with a sugar thermometer in the saucepan. Cook until the temperature reads 90°C/190°F on the thermometer.

Remove from the heat, and allow to cool for 3 minutes.

11. Line your kitchen floor with newspaper, as spinning sugar makes rather a mess. Brush a broom handle with a smear of oil. Place the broom handle so that it sticks out from the side of a bench.

12. To make spun sugar you will need a suitable whisk. To make one, cut off the ends of an old whisk with pliers. This newly-made utensil can then be used time and again to make spun sugar.

13. Dip the spun-sugar whisk into the melted sugar. Flick the whisk over the broom handle so that the melted sugar falls in thin hair-like strands, creating a candy floss effect. Repeat this process until you have used up most of the sugar. Be careful as the sugar is very hot.

14. Roll 4 small balls of spun-sugar between your hands to decorate the dessert.

15. Spoon a pool of raspberry sauce onto the centre of 4 plates or, if you are feeling more ambitious, pipe a flower pattern with piping jelly or melted chocolate. Flood with raspberry sauce.

16. Scoop 4 balls of chocolate mousse with an ice cream baller, and place these balls of mousse in the centre of each flower pattern. Decorate each ball of mousse with 10 pastry leaves.

17. Top with the prepared spun-sugar. Decorate with raspberries and mint sprigs. Dust each plate with icing sugar, and serve immediately.

Lotus Analise

TOFU ICE CREAM

Serves 6
Preparation time: 15 minutes
Freezing time: 4 hours

450 g (15 oz) banana flesh
150 g (5 oz) soft tofu
50 g (2 oz) roasted peanuts
100 ml (3¹/2 oz) fresh orange juice
2 tablespoons honey

This ice cream is best eaten the same day it is made.
1. Cut the bananas and tofu into small pieces.
2. In a liquidizer, blend the roasted peanuts, orange juice and honey. Liquidise to a pulp. Pour into a food processor, scraping out every last drop of mixture with a rubber spatula.
3. Add the diced bananas and tofu, and blend to a smooth paste.
4. Pour into a suitable container, and put in the freezer for 4 hours until frozen, but not solid.
5. Scoop into balls, and serve as it is or with a warm dessert.

SESAME AND POPPY SEED BISCUITS

Makes 40
Preparation time: 10 minutes
Cooking time: 6–8 minutes for each tray

150 g (5 oz) icing sugar
65 g (2¹/2 oz) unsalted butter, softened
175 g (6 oz) plain flour, sifted
1 teaspoon ground ginger
a pinch of salt
4 egg whites
¹/2 tablespoon sesame seeds
butter or sunflower oil for greasing
1 tablespoon poppy seeds

These biscuits are as thin and light as a feather.
1. Place the icing sugar and butter in a medium-size mixing bowl. Using your hand, whip the two together until the butter becomes lighter in both texture and colour.
2. Add the flour, ginger, salt and egg whites to the butter mixture, and continue beating using your hand until the mixture is perfectly smooth. Cover the biscuit mixture with a tea towel and rest it for 30 minutes.
3. Preheat the oven to Gas Mark 5/190°C/375°F.
4. If using non-stick baking sheets, simply spread on thin 10 cm (4-inch) circles of biscuit mixture using a spatula. Otherwise well-grease your baking sheets with butter or sunflower oil before spreading on the biscuit mixtures.
5. Once the biscuits are spread, sprinkle them liberally with sesame and poppy seeds.
6. Bake for a few minutes until golden, watching them carefully. Remove from the oven and allow to cool before eating.

TIP Should you wish to cook only a few biscuits, the remaining uncooked biscuit mixture will easily freeze for up to a month.

APPLE SNOW

Serves 6
Preparation time: 15 minutes
Cooking time: 15 minutes

6 cooking apples
zest of 1 orange
125 g (4 oz) caster sugar
2 tablespoons water
6 egg whites

1. Peel, core and slice the cooking apples, and place them in a pan with the orange zest, sugar and water.
2. Slowly cook the apples until tender, then pass through a sieve into a clean bowl. Allow the apple purée to become quite cold.
3. Whisk the egg whites by hand or with a food processor until stiff, add the apple purée and continue to beat the mixture until it thickens. Pour or pipe into chilled glasses. Place in the refrigerator for 30 minutes before serving.

TIP Remember to make sure the whisk and bowl are perfectly clean and free from any grease whenever egg whites are whipped. A good tip is always to add a pinch of salt to the egg whites.

SWEET DUMPLINGS

Serves 4–5
Preparation time: 10 minutes
Cooking time: 20 minutes

30 g (1¼ oz) lard or vegetable fat
200 g (7 oz) caster sugar
220 g (8¾ oz) freshly grated coconut
125 g (4 oz) chopped almonds
220 g (8¾ oz) mashed cooked potato
450 g (15 oz) plain flour
oil for deep-frying
icing sugar to dust
maple syrup (optional)

Although these dumplings are made with the unusual combination of sugar and potato, they are in fact quite delightful, and are warm and hearty to eat in winter when it's cold outside.

1. Place the lard and sugar first in a lightly warmed mixing bowl. Beat for 3 minutes, then add the remaining ingredients and mix well together.
2. Mould the mixture into balls the size of a small egg.
3. Heat the oil until a cube of day-old bread turns golden in a few seconds. Deep-fry the dumplings for 5–10 minutes until cooked right through. Test by cutting one in half and feeling the temperature: it should be hot.
4. Serve the dumplings hot, either dusted with icing sugar, or if you prefer, with maple syrup.

ALMOND JELLY

Serves 4–6
Preparation time: 20 minutes
Cooking time: 10–15 minutes

15 g (1/2 oz) cornflour or potato flour
900 ml (1 1/2 pints) milk
4 egg yolks
120 g (3 1/2 oz) caster sugar
3 sheets or 9 g (1/4 oz) powdered gelatine
1 tablespoon finely chopped almonds
a few drops of almond essence

1. Dilute the potato flour with a little of the milk. Place the remainder in a pan and bring to the boil. Add the diluted potato flour. Lower the heat and simmer for 3–4 minutes.
2. Quickly whisk in the egg yolks and sugar, and stir gently until the mixture thickens a little. Remove from the heat immediately.
3. Melt the gelatine in a little water, and add to the thickened mixture. Pass the mixture through a fine sieve into a clean bowl.
4. Stir in the almonds, and add the almond essence drop by drop, to taste.
5. Allow to cool, then place in the refrigerator to set.

TIP This jelly can just as easily be set in individual serving bowls.

BANANA JELLY

Serves 4
Preparation time: 6 hours, including the setting time
Cooking time: 25 minutes

3 bananas, plus extra to serve
50 g (2 oz) gelatine or 30 g (1 1/4 oz) agar agar, soaked
750 ml (1 1/4 pints) water
1 cinnamon stick
100 g (3 1/2 oz) caster sugar
2 egg whites
100 ml (3 1/2 fl oz) sherry

1. Cook the bananas in their skins in plenty of boiling water for 15 minutes. Remove the banana pulp from the cooked skins, and purée it with a fork.
2. Put the gelatine or agar agar in a pan with the banana, the water, cinnamon stick and sugar. Bring to the boil, then turn down to a simmer. Cook for 10 minutes then allow to cool.
3. Whisk the egg whites to a soft peak and add them to the cold banana mixture. Mix in well.
4. Bring this banana mixture to the boil then turn down to a simmer for 5 minutes.
5. Pass the jelly mixture through muslin cloth into a clean bowl.
6. Pour the sherry into the banana jelly, mix in well then allow the jelly to cool before placing in the refrigerator to set.
7. Serve when set with sliced fresh bananas.

RED BEAN SORBET

Serves 8
Preparation time: 2–3 hours

150 g (5 oz) red bean paste
3 tablespoons mirin
200 ml (7 fl oz) cold water
ice
150 ml (1/4 pint) cream, semi-whipped

1. Place the first 3 ingredients in a small pan, and bring to the boil.
2. Lower the heat until the mixture simmers, then skim the impurities from the surface with a ladle.
3. Remove from the heat and cool over ice until cold.
4. Pour the mixture into an ice cream machine or into a glass bowl, and freeze. As the sides begin to freeze, whisk quickly until smooth and then re-freeze.
6. When the mixture is three-quarters frozen, after about 2–3 hours, fold through the semi-whipped cream.
7. Continue freezing until the sorbet can be scooped into balls using an ice cream scoop or spoon.
8. Serve in cold glass bowls.

PARSNIP AND PECAN CAKE

Serves 6
Preparation time: 20 minutes
Cooking time: 30 minutes

150 g (5 oz) plain flour
2 teaspoons baking soda
1/2 teaspoon five spice powder
150 g (5 oz) grated parsnip
50 g (2 oz) chopped pecan nuts
1/2 teaspoon grated fresh ginger
1 large egg (size 2), beaten lightly
1 tablespoon Kikkoman soy sauce
30 tablespoons sunflower oil
125 g (4 oz) caster sugar
Icing
zest of 1 orange
100 g (3 1/2 oz) cream cheese
2 tablespoons orange juice
175 g (6 oz) icing sugar
2 drops of orange essence

1. Preheat oven to Gas Mark 4/180°C/350°F.
2. Place all the cake ingredients in a large bowl. Mix well together but do not over-mix.
3. Pour into a 20 cm (8-inch) cake tin. Bake in the oven for 25–30 minutes. Check the cake is cooked by inserting a wooden skewer into the centre. If the skewer comes out clean the cake is done. If not, return it to the oven for a few more minutes.
4. When the cake is cooked, allow it to cool a while before turning it out onto a wire cake rack.
5. Cook the orange zest in a microwave or in boiling hot water until soft.
6. Place all the other icing ingredients in a mixing bowl. Beat until light, slowly at first then on a high speed until the mixture has the consistency of buttercream.
7. Using a palate knife or spatula ice the top of the cake. Sprinkle with the cooked orange zest to finish.

DARK CHOCOLATE MOUSSE WITH A BISCUIT BUTTERFLY AND STRAWBERRY SAUCE

Serves 4
Preparation time: 2¹/₂ hours
Cooling time: 15 minutes

Paste
30 g (1¹/₄ oz) icing sugar
30 g (1¹/₄ oz) flour
25 g (1 oz) unsalted butter
1 egg white
1 drop of almond essence
1 teaspoon cocoa (optional)
Mousse
30 g (1¹/₄ oz) caster sugar
2 egg yolks
3 drops of vanilla essence
5 g (7 oz) gelatine, soaked
4 tablespoons milk
175 g (6 oz) dark chocolate
350 ml (12 fl oz) double or whipping cream, semi-whipped
¹/₂ punnet strawberries or raspberries
Sauce
40 g (1¹/₂ oz) strawberries
1 tablespoon caster sugar
To decorate
piping jelly (optional)
4 mint sprigs

1. Preheat the oven to Gas Mark 5/190°C/375°F.
2. Place all the tuille paste ingredients in a food processor or mixing bowl. Mix until all the ingredients form a smooth paste, and rest for 15 minutes.
3. Draw a butterfly in the centre of a piece of plastic or cardboard then, using a sharp knife, cut out the inside of the butterfly, so as to create a stencil. Place the stencil on a greased baking sheet. Using a palate knife, spread the tuille mix over it.
4. Repeat for the remaining portions. Bake in the oven until golden. Remove from the baking sheet using the palate knife, then place over something round so the wings of the butterflies curve.
5. To prepare the mousse, whisk the sugar, egg yolks and vanilla essence together until the sugar dissolves.
6. Melt the soaked gelatine in a microwave or over a low heat until liquid.
7. Heat the milk in a saucepan, add the white chocolate and melt. Remove from the heat. Add the gelatine, then stir in the egg yolk mixture. Pass through a fine sieve into a clean bowl. Allow to cool a little.
8. Fold through the semi-whipped cream, and refrigerate till set.
9. Prepare the sauce by blending the cleaned strawberries or raspberries with a little caster sugar.
10. Pour a little sauce onto each plate or, if you are feeling more ambitious, pipe on the outlines of leaves using the piping jelly or chocolate then fill these in with the strawberry sauce.
10. Using a warm spoon curl the chocolate mousse into 8 olive shapes. Place 2 curls in the centre of each place, then top with the pastry butterflies. Decorate with strawberries or raspberries. The dessert may be dusted with icing sugar if desired. Serve immediately.

JAPANESE INGREDIENTS SUPPLIERS

Ask at your local Asian food shop for the ingredients you need, otherwise the following stock a wide range of Oriental foods.

UK – London

J A Centre
348–356 Regents Park Road
London N3
Tel: 081 346 1042

Furusato
67A Camden High Street
London NW1
Tel: 071 388 3979

Harrods
Brompton Road, Knightsbridge
London SW1
Tel: 071 730 1234

Ise-ya
182 Preston Road, Wembley
London
Tel: 081 908 4530

Ise-ya
18 Queen's Parade
Queen's Drive
London W5
Tel: 081 997 7107

Loo Fung Supermarket
42–44 Gerrard Street
Chinatown, London W1
Tel: 071 437 7332

Miura Foods
B1 Connaught Business Centre
49 Imperial Way
South Croydon, London
Tel: 081 686 5800

Miura Foods
40 Coombe Road
Kingston, Surrey
Tel: 081 549 8076

Ninjin Food Shop, West End
244 Great Portland Street
London W1
Tel: 071 388 2511

Selfridges
400 Oxford Street
London W1A 1AB
Tel: 071 629 1234

See-woo Supermarket
19 Lisle Street, London W1
Tel: 071 439 8325

S W Trading Ltd
18–20 Lisle Street
London WC2
Tel: 071 439 8325

Tsuru-ya
48 Vivian Avenue
Hendon, London NW4

Wing Yip
395 Edgware Road
Staples Corner, London NW2
Tel: 081 450 0422

Yoshino
15–16 Monkville Parade
Temple Fortune
Finchley Road
London NW11
Tel: 081 209 0966

UK – Outside London

Midori
19 Malborough Place
Brighton
Tel: 0273 601460

A & K Mori
196 Heaton Road
Newcastle upon Tyne
Tel: 091 265 9970

Wing Yip
96–98 Coventry Street
Birmingham
Tel: 021 643 8987

Wing Yip
45 Faulkner Street
Manchester
Tel: 061 832 3215

Yours Mikuni-ya
442 Rayners Lane
Pinner, Middlesex
Tel: 081 868 2003

INDEX

Almond jelly 108
Almond and sesame biscuits 103
Apple and rice cake 102
Apple snow 107
aubergine 37, 86, 97
Aubergines with miso 86
avocado 15, 19, 30, 96
Avocado with ginger dressing 30
Avocado soup with toasted
    almonds 19
Baked halibut with soy sauce 59
Banana jelly 108
beef 64, 71, 73, 76
Braised pumpkin 86
Burmese king prawns with a
    roasted garlic dipping sauce
    44
chicken 12, 18, 35, 42, 43, 49,
    62, 66, 67, 68, 70, 71, 75, 76,
    94
Chicken livers with spinach and
    poppy seeds 38
Chicken and spring onion kebabs
    with peanut butter sauce 68
Chicken teriyaki 66
Chilled avocado and chilli soup
    with nachos 15
crab 28, 88, 92
Crab-stuffed lotus root salad 92
Cream of broccoli and lemon
    grass soup 14
Dark chocolate mousse with a
    biscuit butterfly and
    strawberry sauce 110
dashi 1 15, 18, 20, 21, 39, 42, 47,
    96
dashi 2 20, 21, 38
Dashi (1 and 2) 20
Deep-fried cauliflower with lime
    82
Deep-fried tofu with bonito flakes
    and spring onions 91
Dipped tofu 90
Dipping sauce for cold meat 22
Duck breast Japanese-style 63
Egg fried rice 80
Egg noodles fried with vegetables
    82
Egg and tofu curry 80
Far Eastern pork casserole 72
Five spice spare ribs 68
Fresh fruits deep-fried with rain
    noodles 100
Fresh tuna fish marinated with
    mixed herbs and tomatoes 34

Fried celeriac straw 79
Fried leaf spinach 79
Fried rice with crabmeat and
    spinach 88
Fried sweet sesame bites 103
Grapefruit and avocado salad 96
Green bean salad with peanut
    dressing 96
Green-lipped mussels with lemon
    grass and mirin 51
Grilled aubergine with peanut
    sauce 37
Grilled eel 55
Grilled mackerel with ginger 55
Grilled oysters with lemon
    pepper and chèvre 46
Grilled sea urchin 28
ham 30, 39
Hash browns 83
Honeyed chicken and warm
    mangetout 43
Japanese fishcakes 54
Jasmine tea-smoked swordfish 60
lamb 75
Leek and whitebait fritters 38
Lemon soy sauce 21
Lentil soup 19
lobster 16
Lobster soup with a small lobster
    pancake 16
Lotus Analise 104
Maki-Zushi 25
Mandarin pancakes with two
    fillings 74
Mangetout with chilli sauce 87
Marinated beef 71
Marinated chicken steamed in
    saké 62
melon 30, 31
Melon with Parma ham and
    passion-fruit vinaigrette 30
Melon and prawns with sweet
    and sour sauce 31
Miso soup with chicken, okra and
    leek 18
Monkfish and scallop kebabs 50
Nashi sorbet 102
Neck fillet of lamb with spring
    onions, sesame seeds and
    honey 75
Noodle dipping sauce 21
oysters 46, 58
Oyster fondue – Kaki-nabe 58
Pan-fried aubergine salad with
    sweet and sour sauce 97

Parsnip and pecan cake 109
Picasso ice cream 99
Pickled vegetables 98
Plum vinegar 22
Poached chicken dumplings 49
Poached tofu bites 90
pork 66, 67, 68, 70, 72, 74, 76
Pork and shiitaki meatloaf 66
prawns 31, 40, 42, 44, 45, 57
Prawns with chilli sauce 57
Prawn fries 45
Prawn and tofu pâté 31
Red bean rice 87
Red bean sorbet 109
Roast chicken with vegetable-
    filled jacket potatoes 70
Ruby grapefruit with saké, black
    pepper and mint 29
salmon 25, 59
Salmon teriyaki 59
Sardine hors d'oeuvre spread 34
Sashimi 26
Scallop novelty 56
Scallop ravioli with kaffir lime
    sauce 47
Seafood and vegetable tempura
    51
Sesame and poppy seed biscuits
    106
Shiitaki mushroom consommé
    12
Small pea and ham puddings 39
Smoked chicken and sweet
    potato salad 94
Smoked tofu and soy batter bread
    48
Smoked mussel pâté 35
Soba salad 94
Soba salad with ginger 95
Soy beans cooked with chicken
    wings 75
Spiced fish soup 14
Spiced fried beans with ginger 89
Spring salad 95
Squid chrysanthemum 52
Squid with soy sauce 46
Steamed chicken and prawn
    custard 42
Stewed fish-umani 54
Steamed pork in bamboo 70
Steamed white rice 89
Stir-fried beef with chinese leaves
    and oyster sauce 64
Stir-fried spinach and
    beansprouts 88

Stir-fried vegetables 84
Sukiyaki 73
Sushi 23
Sweet dumplings 107
Sweet potato salad with curry
    mayonnaise 98
Sweet potatoes 83
Sweet and sour baby courgettes
    91
Tandoori chicken 71
Tea-smoked duck with pineapple
    and peppercorn dressing 32
Tempura batter 78
Tempura dipping sauce 21
Teppanyaki 76
Terrine of chicken with pickled
    ginger and saké 35
Thai meatballs flavoured with
    kaffir lime leaves and chillies
    67
Tofu ice cream 106
Tonkatsu 67
Tosa soy sauce 22
Trout marinated with lime, black
    pepper and fresh coriander 36
tuna fish 34, 51, 61
Tuna and parrot-fish with burnt
    saffron 61
Turnip and miso soup 15
Vegetable mousses 85
Vegetarian recipes 14, 15, 19, 29,
    30, 37, 48, 78, 79, 80, 82, 83,
    84, 85, 86, 87, 88, 89, 90, 91
Vinegar soy sauce 21
Warm salad of prawn and celeriac
    ravioli 40
Watercress soup 18